The 24-Hour Action Adventure with ChatGPT

Andrew Parry

Published by Andrew Parry, 2025.

THE 24-HOUR ACTION ADVENTURE WITH CHATGPT

First edition. April 8, 2025.

ISBN: 979-8227854346

Written by Andrew Parry.

Table of Contents

Why Action-Adventure Stories Always Hit the Mark

Action-adventure stories are a ride. They're the kind of tales that throw you into a world of danger, excitement, and discovery—usually with a hero you root for, villains you love to hate, and a mission that gets your heart racing. There's something almost primal about this genre. It taps into the deep human desire for thrill and survival, for bravery under fire, for triumph against impossible odds. And let's be real—whether it's Indiana Jones dodging booby traps or Ethan Hunt hanging off the side of a jet, we live for the adrenaline rush that comes with the journey.

So why do these stories never go out of style? Because they deliver what audiences crave across every age group, time period, and platform. They entertain. They inspire. They challenge. They hit emotional chords while keeping us on the edge of our seats. And when done right, they're unforgettable.

There's something about the combination of action and adventure that creates a magic mix. It's not just about explosions or chases—it's the forward motion of the story, the escalation of stakes, and the idea that the protagonist is actively pursuing something that matters. It might be treasure, justice, revenge, or survival, but there's always a goal—and obstacles thrown in the way at every turn. That structure creates an engine that powers the story from beginning to end without ever losing steam.

At its heart, the genre is all about movement and momentum. Action scenes are usually what get people talking—the car chases, the shootouts, the daring escapes—but it's the adventure that keeps the story grounded. Adventure is what fills the story with purpose. Without that adventurous spirit—curiosity, courage, the thirst for something more—you just have noise. What makes the genre so powerful is the emotional connection that emerges from the character's struggle, not just the fireworks around them.

Another reason action-adventure stories work so well is their universal appeal. You can set them in any time or place. Want to send your hero into the depths of a lost temple in Peru? Go for it. Prefer a high-tech spy mission in the Arctic Circle? That works too. These stories adapt beautifully to different cultures, tones, and genres. You can write a modern urban thriller or a fantasy quest with dragons and still be writing an action-adventure. It's flexible but rooted in strong storytelling principles.

The genre also works incredibly well with ChatGPT. That might sound a bit strange at first, but stick with it. Action-adventure thrives on momentum, and when you're writing at speed—say, trying to generate a full story in one day—you need a co-pilot who can keep up. ChatGPT doesn't run out of ideas. It doesn't get tired or second-guess itself. If you say, "Let's brainstorm a list of 20 wild locations for a hidden treasure," it'll give you twenty. If you say, "What if our villain was a rogue archaeologist with a dark past?" it'll riff with you like a writing buddy who's seen every movie ever made. It's fast, flexible, and always ready to help push the story forward.

This is especially useful in a genre where pacing is everything. You don't want to get bogged down worrying about tiny details or second-guessing your plot logic. You want to be in flow, blasting through scenes, writing that cliffhanger ending to your chapter, and riding the momentum from one big moment to the next. ChatGPT helps keep the energy up, suggesting twists, tightening dialogue, and helping you jump over the speed bumps that usually slow writers down.

You might be wondering if the genre has become a little too familiar. After all, haven't we seen it all before? The truth is, familiarity is a strength here. There are expectations that readers and viewers bring into an action-adventure story, and hitting those expectations in fresh ways is exactly what makes the genre satisfying. The ticking clock, the impossible escape, the hero's comeback—these are narrative beats that audiences love. They know when they're coming, but they still want to see how they'll unfold. It's about reinventing the known, not avoiding it.

When you write in this genre, you're not just giving people entertainment—you're giving them an experience. An escape. An emotional release. And if you can do that with characters who feel real, dialogue that crackles, and pacing that doesn't let up, then you've created something people will remember. And you can absolutely do that with the help of ChatGPT.

This book isn't just going to walk you through how to write a decent action-adventure story. It's going to help you write one *fast.* In a single day, from start to finish. That doesn't mean rushing or cutting corners. It means writing with clarity, purpose, and momentum. It means using the tools that work—like ChatGPT—to stay in the flow, stay inspired, and stay on track.

So as we begin this journey together, remember this: action-adventure stories always hit the mark because they're about energy, emotion, and movement. They're about characters pushed to their limits and stories that move like a bullet train. And when you write one in a single focused day, you're channeling the very spirit of the genre. No hesitation. No turning back. Just forward motion, one page at a time.

Let's get moving.

Using ChatGPT as Your Writing Partner-in-Crime

Let's get something out of the way early: ChatGPT is not here to take over your story. It's here to *amplify* your creative energy. Think of it like a stunt double for your brain when it's tired or stuck. It's the co-pilot you never knew you needed—always ready to bounce ideas, test plotlines, suggest dialogue, or even throw in wild twists when your imagination needs a jolt. And when you're writing an action-adventure story in one single day, trust me, having a creative sidekick who never slows down is exactly what you want.

Writing fast doesn't mean sacrificing quality—it means removing friction. That friction is usually caused by overthinking, second-guessing, or just plain old writer's block. But when you've got ChatGPT feeding you ideas faster than you can type, the writing process transforms. You're no longer staring at a blank screen, waiting for the muse to visit. You're in a creative flow that doesn't need permission to go full speed.

The first thing you'll notice when using ChatGPT to write an action-adventure story is how quickly it adapts to your vibe. You might throw it a prompt like, "A hero is dropped into a jungle and must escape armed mercenaries while uncovering the secret of a lost city." Without hesitation, ChatGPT starts building. It'll give you ideas for scenes, characters, weapons, locations, even bits of snappy dialogue. And if something feels off, just ask it to regenerate or give a different version. You're in the driver's seat.

The beauty is in the speed of iteration. In traditional writing, if an idea doesn't quite land, you might agonize over how to fix it. With ChatGPT, you just try again. Want five different ways to open your story with a bang? Ask. Need alternate villain motivations? Done. Not sure how to structure a scene that blends action with a flashback? Let ChatGPT give you three or four options. The possibilities keep flowing, and you never lose momentum.

Now, here's where it gets fun. You can train ChatGPT to act like a specific kind of storyteller. Tell it you want the tone of a '90s action flick, or the gritty feel of a Jason Bourne movie, or even something more tongue-in-cheek like *Romancing the Stone*. It'll follow your lead and match the energy. That means you're not stuck with one flavor—you can explore variations of your story and see what fits best. It's like having a writer's room in your laptop, always available and always throwing out new spins.

This kind of collaboration is especially useful when you're writing action scenes. Ask ChatGPT to describe a hand-to-hand fight in a nightclub, and you'll get choreography, sensory detail, and even emotional beats. Need to describe a chase through a crowded market in Marrakesh? It can layer in atmosphere, locals, obstacles, and that feeling of chaos that makes a chase scene work. You can fine-tune the details later, but having that rich first draft on the page makes a huge difference when you're under a one-day deadline.

It also shines when plotting. You can say, "Give me a three-act structure for an action-adventure story that involves a former spy, a stolen artifact, and a corrupt government agency," and it'll lay out a roadmap. You don't have to stick to every detail, but it gives you a frame to build on. If you get stuck midway through your story, you can zoom in: "What could be a good midpoint twist?" or "How can the hero escape from a mountain fortress without it being too convenient?" ChatGPT gives you options. You pick the one that makes your story sing.

Another major boost comes with dialogue. Action-adventure stories often move fast, and you want dialogue that's punchy, character-driven, and doesn't slow things down. You can type a few lines and ask ChatGPT to rewrite them to sound funnier, darker, more confident, or more desperate. You can even describe the personality of your character and get custom dialogue that fits their voice. It's a shortcut to authenticity, and it saves loads of time.

Then there's the ability to build out the world. Need to name a jungle that sounds mysterious but isn't too cliché? Ask ChatGPT. Need the layout of a booby-trapped temple? It'll sketch one out in words. Want historical flavor to add realism to your treasure-hunting plotline? You'll get background lore that sounds just plausible enough to work. The tool becomes part historian, part geographer, part myth-maker. And when you need to get a thousand words on the page in an hour, that kind of speed and depth is your secret weapon.

Some writers worry that using ChatGPT makes the work less personal or less authentic. But here's the thing: you're still making all the decisions. You're steering the story. You're choosing what to use and what to ditch. You're bringing the emotional core, the vision, and the passion. ChatGPT is just helping you move faster and explore more possibilities in less time. It doesn't replace your creativity—it unlocks it.

It also doesn't hurt that ChatGPT has read everything. Classic adventure novels, blockbuster screenplays, obscure comics—it's been trained on the language and the structure of stories in all their forms. That means it understands pacing, conflict, arcs, reversals, character tension, and more. You can lean on that understanding while you blaze through your draft.

By the end of this process, you won't just have a finished story—you'll have gone through a full creative experience in turbo mode. You'll know what it feels like to think fast, write faster, and trust your instincts. And you'll see how ChatGPT can keep up with you every step of the way.

So buckle up. This isn't a traditional writing journey. This is a creative heist. You and ChatGPT, plotting together, stealing inspiration from the greats, building something daring, explosive, and full of heart. It's time to write the action-adventure story that's been sitting in your imagination for far too long. And you're going to do it in a single day—with your new partner-in-crime.

The Thrill Starts with the Big Idea

The difference between a decent action-adventure story and one that knocks people out of their seats almost always comes down to the core idea. That big hook. That what-if concept that makes your pulse jump before you've even written a single word. It's the moment your imagination says, *"Yes. That's it."* And when you're writing a full story in one day, there's no time to second-guess or go in half-hearted. You need an idea with energy, with forward motion, with danger, urgency, and possibility baked right into its DNA.

That's where the thrill starts—right at the beginning. Not in the first scene, not when the car explodes, not when the villain appears, but the moment you land on that big, juicy premise that makes the whole thing worth writing. Think about some of your favorite action-adventure movies or novels. Whether it's a tomb buried beneath shifting desert sands or a rogue agent framed for a crime they didn't commit, it all begins with a central idea that crackles with potential.

The beauty of working with ChatGPT is that you don't have to wait for the idea to strike like lightning. You can coax it out, play with it, and evolve it in real time. You can say something simple like, "Give me five wild action-adventure premises," and suddenly you've got a menu of starting points. If nothing grabs you, regenerate. Keep regenerating until something hits. Or take two half-decent ones and smash them together into something new. ChatGPT is your idea forge, and it never runs out of fuel.

Let's say you get a concept like "A marine biologist discovers a map hidden in an ancient whale bone leading to a lost underwater civilization." That's got legs—okay, fins. Immediately, you've got setting (ocean), stakes (discovery), mystery (lost civilization), and a protagonist with a reason to chase the unknown. All you need to do now is build the story on top of it. A good action-adventure idea gives you more than one road to run on. It gives you theme, atmosphere, conflict, and momentum. One idea should be able to generate dozens of scenes, a strong villain, and at least three massive action moments.

If your idea feels too quiet, too tame, too familiar—don't toss it out just yet. ChatGPT is ridiculously good at turning up the heat. Ask it, "How can I make this idea more exciting, more cinematic, more dangerous?" And boom—you might go from "treasure hunt in the woods" to "a cursed relic buried beneath a live volcano surrounded by mercenaries." That shift in scale or threat or setting is often all it takes to level up a lukewarm idea into something high-octane.

It's also smart to think about what your idea promises emotionally. Yes, action-adventure stories are driven by spectacle, but they land hardest when the stakes are personal. So while you're cooking up your big idea, ask yourself, "What's this really about?" Is it a redemption story? A story about betrayal? Is the protagonist proving something to themselves, or righting a past wrong? ChatGPT can help you explore the emotional spine of your idea so the action means something deeper.

Another great tactic is to flip familiar tropes. Instead of a rogue archaeologist, what if your hero is a fraud who's pretending to be one? Instead of a top-tier spy, what if your protagonist is a burnout janitor who accidentally uncovers a secret op? These twists inject surprise and freshness. You're still working within the beloved frame of the genre, but you're playing with it, bending it, making it your own.

And here's where ChatGPT can really stretch its legs. Throw in a weird element. Ask, "What if my hero is allergic to the jungle?" or "What if the villain is a cult leader disguised as a reality show host?" These quirky add-ons push your story into territory that hasn't been explored to death. You don't have to go full absurd, but even a little oddness can make an idea stand out and stick in your mind.

The big idea doesn't have to be fully developed before you begin writing. It just has to be exciting enough to power you through the next few hours. The cool thing about writing fast with ChatGPT is that the idea can evolve as you go. You might start writing a treasure hunt and end up with a survival thriller. You might plan for a jungle and end up in Antarctica. Let the story breathe, but always anchor it in that thrilling core concept that made you want to start typing in the first place.

And don't worry if you come up with something that feels a little wild. In fact, wild is good. This is action-adventure—it's supposed to feel over-the-top. Lean into the chaos. If it feels like it might be too big, too crazy, too bold... that probably means you're on the right track. Let ChatGPT help you scale it, organize it, and smooth out the edges, but never tone it down before you explore it fully. You can always rein it in later. Right now, you're chasing excitement.

So as you stare at your blank page and that blinking cursor, remember: the thrill doesn't start when the story begins. It starts the moment you say, "What if..." and something electric answers back. That's your signal. That's the door opening to the ride you're about to take. All you have to do now is buckle in and go for it. And with ChatGPT riding shotgun, you're never writing alone.

Choosing the Right Kind of Action-Adventure

Not all action-adventure stories are created equal. Some are high-octane thrill rides with explosions and chase scenes every ten minutes. Others are slow burns filled with ancient puzzles, secret codes, and ominous ruins buried beneath centuries of silence. Some have spaceships and time machines, others have motorbikes and machetes. Picking the right kind of action-adventure story is about finding the flavor that excites *you*—the one that gets your creative gears turning and your fingers itching to type. Because once you've locked into the right type, the writing flows like you've already seen the movie in your head.

The genre is broad, and that's one of its superpowers. You can blend it with science fiction, historical drama, fantasy, mystery, horror—even romance. It's basically a storytelling engine that lets you set the dials however you want. That freedom is great, but it can also be overwhelming. So, before you start hammering out scenes, you need to choose your lane. Is this going to be a jungle temple kind of adventure, or more of an urban thriller set against the backdrop of a corrupt international syndicate? Or maybe it's a post-apocalyptic desert run, with survival as the main game?

This is where ChatGPT becomes your genre-sorting machine. You can literally ask, "What are 10 types of action-adventure stories?" and you'll get a buffet of choices. Then you can dig deeper. Want a list of the best sci-fi action-adventure plots? You'll get them. Curious about fantasy-based adventures with epic quests? Done. From secret agent thrillers to treasure hunts to stories of fugitives on the run, ChatGPT can help you break the genre down into digestible types so you can find the one that calls to you.

Think about your story's vibe. Are you aiming for something grounded in the real world with a gritty tone? That's more your spy or military thriller territory. Are you leaning toward something pulpy, fun, and globe-trotting? Hello, lost cities, ancient maps, and mysterious artifacts. If you're more into dark conspiracies and hidden truths, maybe your story veers toward the paranoid thriller, with quiet moments of intensity interrupted by bursts of chaos. Or maybe you want to stretch into the supernatural, with hidden realms, magical relics, or cursed lands. Whatever feels exciting to you is probably the right direction to go.

It also helps to think about your hero. The kind of action-adventure story you write is often shaped by who's at the center of it. A professional thief is going to take you into heist territory. A down-on-their-luck explorer opens the door to lost-world plots. A disgraced government agent could point toward a redemption arc full of espionage and betrayal. Ask yourself, "What is my protagonist built for?" or even better, "What kind of story would push them to the edge?" Because that's where the fun really begins—where capability collides with chaos.

And don't forget tone. Do you want this to be intense and serious, like *The Bourne Identity*, or over-the-top and fun, like *The Mummy*? Do you want to write a morally complex story like *Mad Max: Fury Road*, or a light-hearted adventure like *National Treasure*? Tone sets expectations. It informs your dialogue, your pacing, even how you describe a punch to the face. ChatGPT is great at helping with tone shifts—if you start too heavy and want to lighten it up, just ask for rewrites in a different style. You can try several takes on the same scene and see what sticks.

Another thing to consider is how the adventure unfolds. Is it a quest with a clear destination and a series of escalating obstacles? Or is it more of a survival story where your character has to navigate shifting dangers with no real roadmap? Maybe it's a revenge tale with a deeply personal goal at its center. Maybe it's a race against time, with something catastrophic about to happen unless your hero stops it. ChatGPT can help structure each of these story types with different beats and turning points. Once you choose your template, you can plug in your specifics and go.

Location also plays a massive role in defining the sub-genre. Action-adventure stories are usually tied to place. A crumbling Mayan temple, a remote Arctic research station, a neon-drenched Tokyo alleyway, or a spaceship orbiting Jupiter—each comes with its own tone, stakes, and visuals. Think about where your story takes place and let it help shape the kind of action you write. Different environments create different kinds of danger and different challenges for your characters. Ask ChatGPT to generate unique or unexpected settings for your chosen sub-genre, and you might end up with something fresh that grabs the reader right away.

There's also the option to combine genres. That's where you can get really creative. An action-adventure wrapped in a love story. A mystery set inside a survival thriller. A sci-fi plot that unfolds like a classic treasure hunt. Mashups can be some of the most satisfying to write because they allow you to play with genre conventions while keeping readers guessing. If you're not sure how to blend tones, ChatGPT can offer outlines, tropes, and examples from film and literature that'll show you how others have done it well.

Most importantly, choose a kind of action-adventure story that you genuinely *want* to spend a day inside. Don't pick something just because it's trendy or sounds cinematic. Pick something that sparks your curiosity. Something that makes you want to know what happens next, even if you haven't written a word yet. That excitement will carry through the writing process. You'll feel it in the scenes, and the reader—or viewer—will feel it too.

You don't have to figure it all out before you write. Sometimes the right kind of action-adventure story reveals itself as you go. You might start with a jungle escape and realize halfway through that what you're really writing is a redemption arc in disguise. You might think it's about the treasure, but it turns out to be about a character reclaiming their identity. That's all part of the fun. But getting the direction right at the start can save you time and give you a clear runway to get that story off the ground.

So take a breath. Ask yourself what kind of story you'd love to write if there were no limits. Then tell ChatGPT. You'll be surprised what you two can come up with.

Thinking Backwards: Starting from the Climax

There's a secret weapon most action-adventure writers don't talk about enough—and that's writing the story backward. Not literally typing your scenes in reverse, but starting the entire process by imagining the climax first. That explosive, emotional, high-stakes scene where everything collides, the hero faces their biggest challenge, and the story finally delivers the punch it's been building toward. The climax is where the soul of your story lives, and when you start from there, you write with purpose.

The idea is simple. Instead of wandering through the jungle of ideas hoping to stumble onto a finale, you build the ending first—then reverse engineer the entire adventure to get there. This technique keeps the plot tight and focused, and when you're writing a full story in one day, it's an absolute time-saver. You never get lost wondering what it's all building toward, because you already know.

Let's look at why this works so well, especially in the action-adventure genre. These stories thrive on momentum. Every scene needs to be driving somewhere. When you don't know where that somewhere is, it's easy to stall, or worse, write filler. But when you've got a clear vision of the climax—a helicopter dangling off a cliff, a villain triggering a global virus, a hero choosing between revenge and redemption—you suddenly know what kind of build-up your story needs. Every action, every clue, every choice your hero makes is pointing toward that moment.

Say your ending is a massive underground fight beneath a crumbling ancient temple. You now know your story needs to introduce that temple early, hint at its significance, build toward that location, and maybe layer in an escape plan that gets shattered just before the final scene. Knowing the climax means knowing what to foreshadow. It lets you sprinkle clues, stakes, and tension in a way that feels natural and smart.

You can get ChatGPT to help you build this backwards map. Start by asking something like, "Give me five potential climaxes for an action-adventure story involving a lost city and a double-crossing partner." You'll get dramatic, cinematic options. Choose one that makes your brain light up, then ask, "How can I plot the story backward from this moment?" Boom—now you're working like a screenwriter with the ending locked and loaded.

Thinking backward also makes your characters sharper. Once you know how your protagonist ends the journey—wounded, victorious, transformed—you can trace their emotional arc with precision. If the climax has your hero finally trusting someone after years of isolation, then earlier scenes should show their distrust, their reluctance to open up, and the events that start chipping away at their armor. That way, when the big moment hits, it lands harder because the emotional groundwork has been laid.

The same goes for the villain. What's their role in the climax? Are they trying to escape justice? Destroy a city? Prove a twisted point? When you know what their endgame is, you can thread their presence through the story with clarity. They don't just pop up when it's convenient—they're working in the background the whole time, getting closer to their own goals until the final confrontation.

Another reason this works brilliantly with ChatGPT is because of how easily you can experiment. If you're not sure which climax is right, test out a few. Ask for alternate endings. Run simulations. "What if the hero dies saving the villain?" or "What if the treasure turns out to be a trap?" ChatGPT will help you see the domino effect each choice creates. Once you land on the right one, the story writes itself—because now you're just building the path toward that already-satisfying destination.

One thing that happens when you don't think backward is that you risk meandering. You write cool scenes, but they don't add up. Action-adventure stories can't afford that. They're built on cause and effect. Every decision your characters make should push them toward the final showdown. That's what keeps the pacing tight. That's what makes readers or viewers feel like everything is leading to something epic. And you only get that kind of momentum if you know what you're aiming for.

This approach also saves you from having to rewrite your entire second half. One of the most common reasons writers get stuck halfway through a story is because they realize their ending doesn't match the setup. But if you start with the ending, you're reverse-engineering with confidence. You already know what threads need to be woven in. You already know what clues to drop. You already know what kind of action the story demands.

It doesn't mean the rest of the story is predictable. On the contrary, it often makes the journey more creative. With the destination locked, you're free to experiment with how your characters get there. Will they travel by plane, boat, camel, or bare feet? Will they face natural disasters or political conspiracies? You can go wild with set-pieces and challenges because you always have that magnetic pull of the climax keeping the story aligned.

So let's put it into action. Right now, imagine the last ten minutes of your movie, or the final chapter of your novel. Picture the setting, the danger, the emotional tension. Who's there? What's at stake? What decision is being made? What blows are being traded? Write that scene in rough form or outline it with ChatGPT. Then, ask yourself what had to happen to bring those characters to that moment. What did the hero need to lose? What had to go wrong before this could go right?

Suddenly, the fog lifts. You see the shape of your story. And once that shape is clear, writing the rest of it—fast, bold, and full of energy—becomes a lot less daunting. The climax is your compass. You don't have to be afraid of getting lost anymore. You're just carving the fastest, most thrilling path from page one to the finish line.

So trust your ending. Let it lead you. And let ChatGPT help you build the ride.

World-Building without Getting Lost in the Details

Action-adventure stories thrive on the world they take place in. Whether it's the bustling streets of a futuristic mega-city, the scorching sands of an ancient desert, or the icy expanse of a secret arctic facility, the setting isn't just background—it's part of the story's pulse. But when you're writing a full story in one day, getting bogged down in endless world-building details is a trap you don't want to fall into. The goal isn't to build a world so intricate it needs its own encyclopaedia—it's to create just enough of the world to make your story feel real, vivid, and full of possibilities.

There's a balance to hit here, and ChatGPT makes it a lot easier. World-building should serve your characters and your plot, not the other way around. You're not writing a guidebook—you're building a playground. You don't need to explain the history of an ancient temple in ten pages. You just need to give us enough sensory details so we *feel* the age, the mystery, the threat. Crumbling stone, vines swallowing old symbols, echoing chambers—those kinds of details make a place come alive. And the best part is, you don't have to invent it all from scratch. You can ask ChatGPT for help.

Let's say your story involves a lost jungle city. You can ask ChatGPT, "Describe a lost city hidden in the Amazon jungle," and it will give you texture—weather, architecture, strange fauna, mythological elements. If it spits out too much, just say, "Make it simpler and more grounded," or, "Add a sense of danger and mystery." You're not hunting for paragraphs of lore—you're searching for atmosphere. For story fuel. Because that's what the world should give you: a place where story happens naturally.

World-building also isn't just about places—it's about rules, cultures, and dangers. What makes this world different from our own? Is there a corrupt political force behind the action? A hidden society with a code of honor? A long-forgotten curse influencing events from the shadows? You only need to hint at these things, not explain them in full. A few well-placed details give your world depth without turning your story into a textbook.

You can use ChatGPT like a location scout. Ask it to list unique settings for a final showdown. Ask it for environmental obstacles for each act of your story. Say something like, "What would be a cool location for a motorcycle chase that's not a city?" or "Give me three dangerous paths through a mountain range." Each answer can open a new door for action scenes, emotional beats, and plot turns—all without spending hours doing research or designing fictional maps.

Keep in mind, readers or viewers of action-adventure stories don't need to understand everything about your world—they just need to trust that *you* do. And a confident voice with clear, purposeful description does exactly that. When you throw your hero into a smuggler's den carved into a cliffside monastery, don't pause to explain the monastery's history. Show the flickering candlelight, the monks watching silently, the faint hum of black-market machinery behind the altar. The details you choose *show* the world rather than *tell* it, and that makes it immersive.

Another trick is to build your world around your plot. Instead of designing the world first and then figuring out what story to tell, let the story's needs determine what the world should be. If your climax is a foot chase through an abandoned luxury hotel during a sandstorm, ask, "What kind of world would that exist in?" Maybe it's a city that was evacuated after a chemical leak, or a ghost town buried by a freak desert storm. Start small, build only what you need, and layer in cool stuff that adds danger, mystery, or flavor.

This also applies to technology and gear. If you're writing modern or near-future action, you might be tempted to dive deep into gadgets, vehicles, and weapons. That's fine—just don't let it eat the story. Ask ChatGPT for a list of cool but plausible spy tools or jungle survival gear. Use what serves the scene and discard the rest. The tech is only exciting if it leads to thrilling outcomes or tense complications. Don't explain how the grappling hook works—just show it snapping into stone while the hero dangles over a pit of snakes.

Another way to stay on track is to tie your world-building to your characters. What part of this world has personal meaning to the hero? What place reminds them of their past? What space feels like a trap, a haven, a turning point? When the world reflects or challenges the character emotionally, it does double duty—it builds the world and deepens the story at the same time. And you can ask ChatGPT for that too. Try prompts like, "Design a setting that reflects a character's fear of failure," or "Describe a location that forces the hero to confront their past."

When you're writing on a tight schedule, like in a one-day blitz, your world-building needs to be fast, flexible, and story-driven. Don't create an entire civilization—create a single moment, a single place, a single rule that opens the door to conflict or wonder. Focus on what your characters *see*, *hear*, and *feel* in the moment. That's the stuff readers remember. Not the backstory of a pirate empire, but the way the floorboards creak as your hero tiptoes through a storm-wracked galleon with a ticking bomb in their backpack.

And remember—if you find yourself falling down the world-building rabbit hole, pull back. Ask yourself, "Does this add energy to the story?" If the answer is no, cut it or trim it way down. ChatGPT can help you tighten bloated exposition and find the one line that says more than a paragraph ever could. That's the art of world-building at speed.

So world-build smart. Build only what your story needs. Make it bold, make it believable, and then get back to the action. Because in an action-adventure tale, the world should be a character in the background—dangerous, mysterious, beautiful—but never louder than the story charging through it.

Designing High-Stakes Plots with ChatGPT

High-stakes plots are the beating heart of every great action-adventure story. If the stakes aren't intense, personal, or urgent, then no amount of explosions, car chases, or crumbling temples is going to keep the audience glued. People stay invested in a story not just because things are happening, but because *something important is on the line.* A great action-adventure plot doesn't just throw the hero into danger—it forces them to risk everything for something they care about. That's where the tension comes from. That's where the thrill lives.

Designing that kind of story from scratch can feel like a lot, especially if you're trying to pull it off in a single day. But here's the good news: you've got ChatGPT as your plotting partner, and it's ridiculously good at generating high-stakes story frameworks that you can shape, stretch, or flip on their head. You're not staring at a blank page—you're standing at the helm of a machine that spits out plotlines faster than you can scroll.

So, how do you build a high-stakes plot using ChatGPT? You start by identifying what kind of stakes you want. There are generally three levels of stakes in an action-adventure story: personal, relational, and global. Personal stakes might involve the hero's survival, redemption, or secret past. Relational stakes involve someone close to the hero—like a kidnapped sibling, a betrayed mentor, or a lost love. Global stakes are your big ones—stop the virus, recover the weapon, save the world.

Now here's where it gets fun. You don't have to pick just one. The most gripping stories often layer all three. Ask ChatGPT something like, "Give me a high-stakes action-adventure plot that combines personal, relational, and global stakes." It might return something like: "A disgraced former pilot must rescue his estranged daughter, who holds the key to a deadly satellite weapon about to be launched by a rogue state." That's a plot with teeth. The personal redemption arc, the father-daughter relationship, and the world-in-danger urgency all collide in a way that gives your story depth and momentum.

ChatGPT can also help you scale the stakes. Maybe your original idea feels too small. Just ask, "How can I raise the stakes in this story?" Let's say your plot involves a treasure hunt. ChatGPT might suggest adding a rival team with deadly motives, or a ticking clock that forces the hero to make impossible choices. Maybe the treasure is tied to an ancient virus that could be unleashed if opened incorrectly. Suddenly, your story isn't just about gold—it's about survival, betrayal, and sacrifice.

Structure is another place ChatGPT shines. You can say, "Outline a three-act high-stakes action-adventure plot involving a hidden island and a rogue scientist." It'll give you a beginning, middle, and end—with escalating danger and turning points built in. If you want to go deeper, ask for scene breakdowns. Say, "What are 10 key scenes for this kind of plot?" And there they are—set pieces, emotional moments, reveals—all ready to be customized and filled out.

You can even workshop twists on the fly. If the stakes are too predictable, tell ChatGPT, "Add an unexpected betrayal at the midpoint," or "What if the villain isn't who we think it is?" The AI will adjust the plot, give you new angles, and keep your story fresh. And when you're working under time pressure, having a tool that can pivot instantly is a massive creative boost.

Another great approach is asking ChatGPT to combine influences. You could say, "Give me a high-stakes plot that mixes *The Fugitive* with *Tomb Raider*," or "Combine *Indiana Jones* with *Die Hard*." The AI will mash up themes, tone, and plot beats into something wild and full of energy. Sometimes it'll be exactly what you need. Sometimes it'll be weird and unexpected—which can be even better. A strange idea can become your story's secret weapon.

If you're trying to make the stakes feel more emotional—because action alone isn't enough—ask ChatGPT for help connecting the plot to the protagonist's inner world. "How can I tie the external danger in this story to the hero's personal journey?" That's how you take a plot from surface-level fun to something with weight. Maybe the hero's trying to stop the same kind of disaster that once destroyed their hometown. Maybe they're trying to protect someone the way no one protected them. When the stakes reflect a deeper truth, the story hits harder.

Another simple but powerful prompt: "What's the worst thing that could happen to my protagonist right now?" Keep asking that throughout the story. The higher the stakes, the more pressure the hero is under. And when a character is under pressure, they make bold, risky, emotional choices—the kind of choices that make scenes unforgettable.

As you plot, you'll start seeing how all the moving parts line up—the world, the stakes, the antagonist, the pacing, and the emotional arc. Don't feel like you have to nail it all in one shot. ChatGPT is a great place to test out variations. "What if the hero's goal changes in Act 2?" or "What if the person they're saving doesn't want to be saved?" These kinds of questions add complexity and tension without slowing you down.

By the time you're done plotting, you'll have a story that doesn't just move—it roars. A story with consequences. A story where the hero's choices matter, where danger builds, and where the payoff at the end actually feels earned. That's the magic of a high-stakes plot. And you don't need weeks of outlining or a whiteboard covered in string to get there. You've got ChatGPT. All you need is a killer idea, a willingness to explore it from every angle, and the guts to write fast and bold.

So don't overthink it. Throw in your wildest concepts, test your stakes, and let the story take off. With ChatGPT in your corner, designing a high-stakes action-adventure plot doesn't have to be complicated—it just has to be thrilling.

Character First: Creating a Hero Worth Following

Action-adventure stories live or die on the strength of their main character. Sure, people come for the wild stunts, mysterious locations, and ticking time bombs—but they *stay* because they care about who's in the driver's seat. You could have the most explosive plot in the world, but if your hero is bland or forgettable, no one's going to stick around. That's why the first real priority—before the treasure, the villain, the secret base, or even the first scene—is crafting a hero that the audience actually wants to follow.

Creating that kind of character doesn't mean they have to be perfect. In fact, far from it. The best action-adventure protagonists are often messy, flawed, or carrying some kind of emotional baggage. They've got something to prove, something to protect, something they lost—or something they fear losing. That's what gives the story its emotional gravity. That's what turns cool action into meaningful action. You're not just watching someone leap across rooftops; you're watching someone fight for redemption, for justice, for family, or sometimes just for survival.

When building your protagonist with ChatGPT, the first thing to do is start with their core. What kind of person are they—on a gut level? Are they cynical or hopeful? Lone wolf or team player? Former hero or reluctant one? You can literally ask ChatGPT, "Give me five action-adventure protagonists with different personality types," and it will give you a spread—from the gruff ex-mercenary who's haunted by a past mission, to the overconfident treasure hunter who's never faced real loss. Pick one that feels right or combine traits until someone interesting starts to emerge.

Next, ask: what's their emotional wound? That's where the story really begins. Maybe they've been betrayed by someone they trusted. Maybe they failed to save someone and can't forgive themselves. Maybe they grew up never feeling good enough, and this mission is their chance to finally prove something—to the world or to themselves. This wound becomes the engine for their growth. ChatGPT can help you explore this by asking, "What kind of emotional backstory would create a reluctant hero?" or "What trauma might drive someone to seek danger instead of safety?"

Then think about what your hero *wants* versus what they *need*. What they want is usually external—find the artifact, save the hostage, clear their name. But what they need is internal—maybe they need to let go of control, or learn to trust others, or face the truth they've been avoiding. The magic happens when the action forces them to confront the need. That's the character arc. And you can build it scene by scene using ChatGPT prompts like, "How can this mission force my hero to face their fear of failure?" or "What situations would challenge a control freak hero?"

Don't forget about skills and weaknesses. Your hero should be competent—but not invincible. Give them strengths that help them survive, but weaknesses that create tension. A genius codebreaker might freeze under pressure. A hardened soldier might struggle with emotional decisions. These contradictions make them human. You can ask ChatGPT to generate combinations like, "Give me a skilled adventurer with a personal flaw that causes conflict," and you'll get suggestions that instantly spark scenes and subplots.

Another big one: motivation. Why is your hero doing this at all? Are they being paid? Blackmailed? Are they trying to protect someone? Redeem themselves? Or are they chasing something they don't even fully understand yet? The deeper the motivation, the more compelling the action becomes. If they're only in it for the money, you've got a shallow story. But if they're risking everything to stop the villain who once destroyed their family, or trying to recover something stolen from their culture, now you've got real stakes.

Now let's talk charisma. Your hero doesn't need to be funny, but they need to be *watchable*. Maybe they're stoic and intense, like John Wick. Maybe they're fast-talking and unpredictable, like Jack Sparrow. Or maybe they're everyman types who rise to the occasion, like John McClane. You can use ChatGPT to find that sweet spot. Try prompts like, "What personality traits would make an action hero instantly engaging?" or "Write sample dialogue for a sarcastic hero with a good heart." You'll get instant flavor that helps lock in their voice.

Relationships are another great tool to make your hero shine. Who do they care about? Who challenges them? Who do they protect, or clash with, or rely on when things get rough? Even if you're writing a solo adventure, building out a few key relationships makes your hero richer. Think of Indiana Jones and his father. Or Lara Croft and her tech team. These connections reveal aspects of the hero that we wouldn't see if they were alone the whole time. You can ask ChatGPT to generate relationship dynamics: "Give me three supporting characters who can challenge my hero's beliefs."

And don't forget about transformation. Your hero should end the story different than they began. Maybe they were selfish and learned to sacrifice. Maybe they were broken and found healing. Maybe they were angry and found peace—or peace and found their anger when it mattered most. Ask ChatGPT to help sketch a before-and-after. "Describe how my hero changes between the beginning and end of the story." You'll start to see the emotional roadmap forming under the action.

Once you've got your character, keep checking in with them as you write. If a scene feels flat, ask yourself: what does this moment reveal about the hero? What are they learning, or avoiding, or confronting? Is this choice consistent with their personality? Are they growing—or are they stuck, and if so, why? ChatGPT can help you realign scenes with the arc by prompting character beats or reactions that feel real.

In the end, your audience might come for the stunts and spectacle, but they'll stay because they care about who's in the center of it all. Give them a hero who bleeds, doubts, cracks jokes, faces fears, and keeps going anyway—and they'll follow that character through fire. You don't need to build a superhero. You need to build a human being worth rooting for. And with ChatGPT helping you sculpt the flaws, the charm, the drive, and the growth—you're building someone unforgettable. Someone we want to watch win. Or lose. Or just survive one more day.

Building a Villain That Demands a Showdown

Every great action-adventure story has one thing in common: a villain who demands a showdown. Not just a generic bad guy with a gun or a power-hungry warlord with a plan. We're talking about a real, flesh-and-blood character who forces the hero to rise, fall, and fight like hell to overcome them. A villain who isn't just in the way—they *are* the way. The way to growth, to redemption, to a truth the hero would never have faced otherwise. That's the kind of antagonist that sticks with us long after the credits roll or the final page turns.

So how do you build a villain like that—especially when you're writing an entire story in one day? Easy. You let ChatGPT help you explore the kind of character who's as complex, compelling, and dangerous as your hero deserves. Because the truth is, the stronger your villain, the more satisfying your story. They're the storm that drives everything. And if you do it right, your villain isn't just a person—they're a mirror. They reflect your hero's flaws, fears, and failures. And in that final face-off, they force the hero to confront all of it.

Start by figuring out what your villain *wants*. Not just what they do, but what's driving them. Do they crave power, vengeance, chaos, recognition, control? Why? What made them that way? Maybe they lost everything and now believe the world deserves to burn. Maybe they're a zealot, convinced they're saving humanity. Maybe they were once just like the hero but took a different path when everything fell apart. You can ask ChatGPT, "Give me five villain motivations that are personal and emotional," and you'll get layers instead of clichés. That's the difference between a forgettable baddie and someone who gets under the audience's skin.

Then think about how your villain relates to your hero. The best action-adventure stories often have a villain who is a twisted reflection of the protagonist. Think of *Skyfall*—Silva is a former agent, like Bond, but broken by betrayal. Or *Black Panther*—Killmonger wants justice but takes it too far. The contrast adds emotional heat. You're not just watching two people fight—you're watching two worldviews collide. Ask ChatGPT, "What kind of villain would challenge a hero who's afraid to trust others?" and it'll give you an antagonist designed to press exactly the right buttons.

Personality matters too. Not every villain needs to be cool, slick, and collected. Some are quiet and calculating. Some are theatrical and unpredictable. Some are charming on the surface but ice-cold underneath. What matters is consistency. If your villain believes in something, they should follow it through. If they manipulate people, let them manipulate everyone. ChatGPT can help you define the voice and tone of your antagonist. Ask, "Write dialogue for a villain who believes order must be restored at any cost," and you'll start to see their presence take shape in words.

It's also essential to give your villain power. Not just physical or tactical power, but *narrative* power. They should be capable of disrupting the hero's plans, turning allies against them, even winning for a while. If your villain doesn't feel like a real threat, then the showdown won't mean anything. You can ask ChatGPT, "How can my villain gain the upper hand at the end of Act Two?" and it'll offer you clever ways to put your hero in checkmate. And then you get to figure out how they'll claw their way back.

Another key trait of a great villain is presence. Even if they're not in every scene, their shadow should be. Their choices should ripple through the story. Their plans should affect the world. You want your audience to *feel* them, even when they're not on the page or screen. That's how you build dread. That's how you make the final confrontation inevitable. Ask ChatGPT to brainstorm "ways to show a villain's influence even when they're off-screen," and it'll give you ideas for scenes, messages, betrayals, or consequences that constantly raise the stakes.

Don't forget to give your villain their own arc. They may not "grow" in the same way as your hero, but they should evolve. They may start in control and end desperate. They may begin in the shadows and rise into full view. The arc adds momentum and makes them feel like a living character, not just a static obstacle. You can ask ChatGPT for help with this too. Try, "Describe the emotional arc of a villain who believes they're the real hero," and you'll start seeing how your antagonist can shift and unravel over time.

Designing the final showdown is another moment where your villain really shines. This isn't just a fight—it's the culmination of everything both characters believe. If your villain is cold and controlled, maybe they lose it at the end. If your hero has avoided confrontation, maybe this is where they step up. You can ask ChatGPT, "Give me three endings where the hero defeats the villain but loses something important," and you'll find a dozen different ways to make the climax matter.

And sometimes, the villain doesn't die. Sometimes they win. Or escape. Or plant the seed for the next big story. That lingering presence can give your action-adventure tale a haunting aftertaste. And you guessed it—ChatGPT can help you with those twists too.

The point is, don't treat your villain like a box you check on the story checklist. Build them with the same energy and imagination you put into your hero. Give them purpose. Give them moments of clarity, even humanity. Let them *earn* the showdown. Because the more formidable your villain, the more heroic your hero has to become.

So ask the big questions. What would this villain die for? What would they never forgive? What line would they never cross—until they do? And how does everything they believe bring them crashing into the path of your protagonist?

With ChatGPT guiding your brainstorms, testing your ideas, and sharpening your character design, you'll have everything you need to craft a villain who isn't just dangerous—but unforgettable. A villain who makes that final showdown not just inevitable... but absolutely necessary.

Supporting Cast that Brings the Fire

Your action-adventure story might orbit around one central hero, but it's the supporting cast that fills the world with heart, humor, betrayal, surprise, and firepower. These characters aren't just background noise or exposition machines—they're the ones who challenge the hero, make the stakes personal, and sometimes even steal the show. You want every supporting character to feel like they've got their own story running just beneath the surface, whether it ever makes it onto the page or screen or not. And when you're writing fast—like one full story in a day—you need a cast that clicks quickly, adds contrast, and creates sparks in every scene.

So where do you start? With roles. Think of the different roles your supporting cast might play. The loyal sidekick, the reluctant ally, the insider with secrets, the mentor with a mysterious past, the comic relief who saves the day without realizing it, the ex who still knows how to push buttons, the double agent, the betrayer, the wild card. You can have just one or two, or a whole team, depending on your story. Either way, they need to earn their place by adding something the hero can't bring alone.

This is where ChatGPT becomes a character factory. You can ask, "Give me five action-adventure supporting characters with contrasting personalities," and you'll get an instant line-up of possibilities. Maybe a by-the-book intelligence officer paired with a reckless thrill-seeker. Maybe a hacker who refuses to leave their van, or a monk with a secret past in black ops. You can refine these on the fly. Want someone older? Younger? From a specific background? Driven by revenge? Disillusioned with the mission? Ask, and ChatGPT gives you options that bring variety and friction.

Friction, by the way, is gold. Great supporting characters don't always get along with the hero. In fact, some of the most memorable dynamics come from conflict. Think of the sarcastic pilot who constantly second-guesses the mission. The hot-headed friend who wants to fight first and think later. The bureaucrat forced into the field who has no idea what they're doing. These characters create opportunities for banter, growth, and tension. Ask ChatGPT for dynamics like, "Give me a character who clashes with my cautious protagonist but ultimately earns their trust."

Every character should have a goal—even the ones in the background. They don't need pages of development, but they should be chasing something. It could be loyalty to someone else, money, revenge, redemption, or even just survival. When supporting characters have agendas, the story feels more alive. The world isn't just reacting to the hero—it's moving on its own. Ask ChatGPT to help you layer this in: "What's a hidden agenda for a supporting character who pretends to help the hero?"

Let's talk about dialogue for a second. One of the fastest ways to make your supporting cast pop is to give them distinct voices. Not everyone should sound like your main character. One might be blunt, another poetic, one constantly nervous, another stoic and unreadable. Use ChatGPT to help you get it right. Say, "Write a scene where a sarcastic sidekick and a no-nonsense hero argue over their next move," and watch the character chemistry jump off the page. You can do this for every major supporting role—test their voice, find their tone, and lock it in.

And don't forget: supporting characters can steal the spotlight in a good way. You want moments where they shine. The sidekick gets to save the hero's life. The quiet one delivers a killer line that breaks the tension. The morally gray character makes a sacrifice no one expected. Ask ChatGPT, "What's a surprising heroic moment for a character who's mostly comic relief?" or "What's a great reveal for a background character with a secret connection to the villain?" You'll get the kind of character beats that add layers to your story without adding bulk.

Another powerful role for your supporting cast is to serve as emotional anchors. They're the ones the hero lets their guard down around. The ones who remind them why they're fighting in the first place. Maybe it's a younger sibling they're protecting, or an old friend who knows the hero's darkest secret. These characters can ground the story emotionally, especially when the action is at full throttle. Ask ChatGPT for emotional dynamics like, "What kind of character could remind my hero what they're fighting for?"

And yes, sometimes supporting characters die. That's the genre. But if they go out, it should matter. Their death should shift the hero, raise the stakes, or change the direction of the story. Don't just throw them away for shock value. Make it personal. Make it mean something. You can ask ChatGPT, "How can the death of a supporting character fuel the hero's final decision?" and you'll get angles that tie everything together emotionally.

Finally, your supporting cast can be used to explore the world. A local guide introduces the culture. A scientist explains the relic's backstory. A rogue pilot gives insight into how the villain's operation really works. These characters allow you to deliver exposition in a natural, engaging way. Instead of info dumps, you get color, perspective, and history—wrapped in someone the audience already cares about.

The key to building a supporting cast that brings the fire is to make sure each one feels essential. They're not decorations. They're not plot devices. They're people who've chosen—or been forced—to ride alongside your hero. They bring skills, conflict, personality, emotion, and unexpected turns. When they speak, it matters. When they act, it changes something. When they're in danger, we feel it.

So don't treat them like extras in the background. Build them with intention. Give them voices that clash and harmonize with your lead. And let ChatGPT help you brainstorm the relationships, roles, and reveals that make them unforgettable. Because when your supporting characters are strong, your action-adventure story isn't just a solo journey—it's an ensemble that pulses with life, heat, and, yes—fire.

Crafting the Perfect Set-Piece Moment

Every action-adventure story needs set-pieces—those big, unforgettable moments where everything explodes, tumbles, races, or fights its way into cinematic history. These are the scenes your audience talks about afterward. They're the adrenaline spikes in the pulse of your story. Done right, they're not just cool—they're essential. Set-pieces are story beats dressed in spectacle. They serve the plot, shape the character arcs, and push the tension higher. And if you're writing your story in one day, you'll need to plan these sequences fast, smart, and with maximum impact.

So what exactly makes a set-piece memorable? It's not just chaos and noise. A great set-piece has clear stakes, character-driven tension, an evolving sequence of beats, and ideally, some kind of twist that surprises the audience. Whether it's a rooftop chase, a collapsing bridge, a midair rescue, or a treasure heist gone sideways, the scene should feel like the hero might not make it—and even if they do, they won't come out unchanged.

Start by asking yourself what's happening in the story at this moment. What's the point of this scene? Are you raising the stakes? Turning the tide? Forcing the hero to face a fear? Introducing a betrayal? Set-pieces are most powerful when they're built on more than just action. They should reveal character under pressure. Think of it this way: the bullets and explosions get our attention, but the choices the character makes in the middle of the chaos—that's what keeps us locked in.

If you're unsure where to place your set-pieces, think of them as the anchors of your story structure. One early on to hook the audience. A big one at the midpoint to flip the story or raise the stakes. One in the final act that becomes the climax or leads directly into it. You don't need a dozen—you need a few excellent ones that elevate your story. And this is where ChatGPT becomes a scene-storming powerhouse.

Let's say your story is set in a crumbling city during a volcanic eruption. Ask ChatGPT, "Give me a set-piece involving a high-speed escape across collapsing rooftops while lava flows through the streets below." You'll instantly get a scene framework packed with tension, visuals, and movement. Or ask for variety: "Give me five original set-pieces for an underwater treasure-hunting story." You'll get a range—from sea creature attacks to claustrophobic caves to betrayal at the decompression chamber.

What's great is you can push and pull the idea. Tell ChatGPT to raise the stakes: "Now add a moral dilemma into that rooftop escape." Maybe the hero sees someone trapped. Do they save them or keep running? Now it's not just action—it's emotion. And that's where set-pieces really start to shine.

A good set-piece also needs escalation. It should start in one place and end somewhere completely different. Think of it like a rollercoaster. The hero thinks they're just retrieving a briefcase from a warehouse—but then the lights go out. Then the building locks down. Then the villain's men arrive. Then the hero is cornered—and the only way out is through the ventilation system, which leads to a construction crane hundreds of feet above the ground. Each beat ramps things up, twists the direction, and forces the hero to adapt.

ChatGPT can help you map this out in real time. Ask, "Break this scene into five escalating stages," and you'll get a blueprint you can write from immediately. Then tweak it: make it faster, add emotional stakes, throw in environmental hazards. Maybe it's a storm, a fire, a ticking clock. The danger should grow, the options should shrink, and the pressure should mount.

You should also design your set-piece around who your hero is. If your protagonist is resourceful, make them use the environment in creative ways. If they're haunted by a traumatic memory, maybe this location brings it roaring back. If they've always played it safe, this is the moment they jump. Literally. Ask ChatGPT, "What kind of set-piece would challenge a character who fears heights?" or "Design a set-piece that forces my reckless character to slow down and think." The more personal the challenge, the better the payoff.

Don't overlook the power of surprise. Even in a huge, intense action sequence, you want the audience to feel like they don't know what's coming next. Maybe the villain is waiting at the exit. Maybe the hero reaches the goal—only to realize it's a trap. Maybe the explosion they thought would stop the enemy actually unleashes something worse. ChatGPT is fantastic for this. Ask, "What's a great twist that can happen at the end of a helicopter escape sequence?" and you'll get dozens of curveballs to keep the adrenaline flowing.

Now let's talk about the sensory side. Set-pieces are visual, physical, chaotic—but also textured. What does the character hear? What's the temperature? What obstacles are unexpected? What physical toll does the scene take? Don't just say, "They run through the jungle." Say, "The underbrush cuts their arms, rain soaks their clothes, and the sound of gunfire bounces through the trees." ChatGPT can generate environmental detail quickly and richly. Use it to make the moment feel *there*.

And lastly, remember the exit. How does the set-piece end? Who wins? Who loses? What changes? A perfect set-piece doesn't just get the hero from point A to point B. It changes the equation. Maybe they lose something vital. Maybe they earn someone's trust. Maybe the enemy sees them bleed for the first time. The aftermath should matter. Ask ChatGPT, "What are the emotional consequences of surviving a helicopter crash caused by the hero's mistake?" You'll get insight that ties the spectacle back to the character arc.

In a one-day writing sprint, having a few well-structured set-pieces can give your story backbone. They're the big beats that carry the rest of the narrative. You can build toward them, recover from them, and let your quieter scenes breathe between them. And with ChatGPT on your team, you'll never run dry on ways to make those moments not just big—but unforgettable.

So when in doubt, go bigger. Then go deeper. Let the action reveal something real. Let the danger push your characters further than they thought they could go. That's what a great set-piece does—it turns a scene into a story, and a story into a memory.

Creating an Opening that Pulls Readers In

If there's one part of your action-adventure story that absolutely cannot afford to miss the mark, it's the opening. The first scene. The hook. That very first taste of your world, your protagonist, and the tone of the journey to come. This is where you make your promise to the reader—or viewer. You're saying: *Strap in. This is going to be wild.* And they either believe you and stick around... or they don't. That's why your opening needs to do more than just set the scene. It has to grab the reader by the collar, drop them into the middle of something compelling, and leave them with no option but to keep going.

Now, pulling this off in a one-day writing sprint can seem like a tall order. But here's the trick: don't try to explain everything right away. Don't try to build the entire world in the first three paragraphs or establish every character relationship up front. Instead, throw us into motion. Start with an image, a moment, a decision, a problem already in progress. Open with tension, with motion, with a sense that something is already happening. Then let the rest of the details unravel naturally as the story surges forward.

The best way to do this is to pick the right kind of opening. Action-adventure stories lend themselves well to starting *in media res*—right in the thick of it. Maybe the hero is already on a mission that goes wrong. Maybe there's a chase underway, a theft in progress, a meeting that turns into an ambush. Think of the opening of *Raiders of the Lost Ark*—we don't get a long explanation of who Indiana Jones is. We get a jungle, a booby-trapped temple, a golden idol, and a giant rolling boulder. Within five minutes, we know everything we need to know: this guy takes risks, thinks fast, and gets into trouble.

If you're not sure how to start your own opening scene, this is where ChatGPT becomes a launchpad. Try prompts like, "Give me five action-packed opening scenes for a story about a rogue archeologist," or "Describe an intense first scene for a story set on a hijacked cargo ship." You'll instantly have options that drop you into the story with energy and purpose. If one grabs you, you can then ask, "Expand this into a full opening sequence," and you've got a solid first scene in minutes.

The opening also needs to introduce tone. If your story has a sense of humor, we should get a taste of it right away. If it's gritty and grounded, that should be clear in the first few lines. If it's fantastical or stylized, the opening should drip with those details. Don't save your tone for later. Readers will assume whatever you show them up front is the standard. So don't hold back. Ask ChatGPT, "How can I set a dark, fast-paced tone in my first paragraph?" or "Write a playful opening scene that includes action and banter." Let the style come through with confidence.

You also want to drop in a question early. Not a literal one, but a narrative question. Something the reader needs answered. Why is the protagonist running? What's inside the locked case? Why did the villain say "you'll never make it out alive" before vanishing into the shadows? These questions pull readers forward. Curiosity is as powerful as any explosion. You can ask ChatGPT, "Suggest intriguing mystery elements to include in my story's opening," and it'll give you breadcrumbs to scatter in just the right places.

Now, what about your protagonist? Do they need to show up in the first scene? Usually—yes. If you can introduce your hero doing something that reveals who they are under pressure, even better. Let us see them in action. You don't need to explain their full backstory—just show them making choices. Do they save the innocent bystander or complete the mission? Do they argue with their handler, crack a joke, or go quiet when things get dangerous? You can even ask

ChatGPT, "Write a scene that introduces a hero who's cocky but secretly afraid of failure," and you'll start to see the layers you can reveal right away.

Let's not forget setting. While you don't want to over-describe, you do want to make the world feel real from the first sentence. Give us temperature, atmosphere, texture. Is the story opening on a sweaty rooftop in a neon-lit city? A dusty road with a convoy under attack? A submarine crashing through Arctic ice? Ask ChatGPT for vivid descriptions of your setting in one paragraph. Say, "Describe the opening scene of a thriller set in a remote jungle airstrip," and you'll get a sensory backdrop that gives your characters something to move through.

Another opening approach is the "slow burn that goes boom." You might start quietly—maybe your hero is in disguise, infiltrating a location—and tension slowly builds until the moment explodes. This contrast can be really effective, especially if you want to lull the audience before the action hits hard. ChatGPT can help with pacing that rise in tension: "Write a tense opening that builds to an unexpected shootout."

And don't underestimate how helpful a great line of dialogue can be. A killer first line from your protagonist or villain can set the tone, define character, and make the reader sit up straight. Ask for options: "Give me ten badass opening lines for an action-adventure hero," and you'll probably find something you want to use, twist, or steal outright.

In the end, your opening scene doesn't need to explain everything. It just needs to make a promise. A promise that this story is going to take readers somewhere exciting, dangerous, emotional, and unpredictable. A promise that this hero is worth following. A promise that the world is worth exploring. And with ChatGPT's ability to help you brainstorm scenes, suggest sensory details, build pacing, and test different approaches, you'll never be stuck wondering how to begin.

So grab your hook. Your jungle. Your villain. Your chase. And open the story like the match just hit the fuse. Light it up, let it roar, and trust that if you start strong, the rest of the story will ride the momentum all the way to the end.

Dialogue that Snaps, Moves, and Reveals

Action-adventure stories aren't just about bullets flying and temples collapsing. They're also built on dialogue—tight, sharp, and loaded with purpose. Dialogue is your secret weapon. It makes characters memorable, reveals their motivations, adds tension to a scene, and injects humor or heart when everything's blowing up around them. Great dialogue doesn't just fill space between action scenes—it *is* action in its own right. It can move a story forward faster than a car chase, and when done right, it sticks with your audience just as much as the explosions.

When writing an action-adventure story in a single day, dialogue can become your shortcut to character, pacing, and emotion. But only if you write it right. Lazy dialogue slows things down. Overwritten dialogue makes characters sound like robots. And dialogue that doesn't reveal anything—about the plot, the stakes, or the people talking—is just noise. You want lines that snap with personality, move the story forward, and reveal something important beneath the surface.

So how do you do that at speed? Easy—you let ChatGPT help you break the silence and get the tone exactly right.

Let's start with *snapping*. Snappy dialogue is about rhythm. It's fast, clever, and to the point. Think of the back-and-forth between Han Solo and Princess Leia. Or the sarcastic quips of Indiana Jones. Or the quick-fire banter of a spy team mid-mission. These lines cut through the noise. They keep the reader or viewer hooked. If you want your dialogue to snap, ask ChatGPT, "Write ten one-liners for a cocky hero under pressure," or "Give me fast-paced banter between two rival adventurers." You'll get options you can tweak, blend, or steal outright.

The trick is not to overdo it. Not every line needs to be a zinger. Save the sharpest stuff for when it counts—during a tense stand-off, a moment of panic, or right before something goes boom. Contrast is key. Let your dialogue breathe between punchy moments, and those lines will hit harder.

Now onto *moving*—dialogue that pushes the plot forward. This kind of conversation carries information, changes the game, or drives a decision. It might reveal a plan, expose a lie, deliver a warning, or set a trap. In action-adventure, you don't have time for long philosophical debates. Dialogue should always be working—delivering a clue, shifting an alliance, escalating the stakes.

To do this well, think of every line of dialogue like a fuse. Ask yourself, "What's this line setting up?" or "How does this exchange change what's happening next?" If the dialogue isn't doing that, it's slowing you down. Ask ChatGPT for help: "Write a tense exchange that reveals the villain's next move without stating it directly," or "Give me a dialogue scene where the hero realizes their ally can't be trusted." You'll get something that changes the direction of the story in a matter of lines.

Then there's *revealing*—dialogue that opens up character. The best lines aren't always about plot. They're about who the characters are under the mask. What they fear. What they love. What they regret. A great line can tell us everything about a character's heart without spelling it out. "I don't do rescue missions," says a lot more about a person than a paragraph of backstory. And when that same character later whispers, "I came back for you," it means everything.

ChatGPT is your best tool for exploring these emotional cracks. Try, "Write a scene where the hero tries to hide their guilt in a conversation," or "Give me dialogue where a character reveals their fear through a joke." You'll start to get lines that feel real, not rehearsed. These moments are where the story deepens—and the audience bonds with your characters.

You should also think about *voice*. Each character needs to sound like themselves. A stoic mercenary won't talk like a fast-talking street thief. A refined villain won't use the same vocabulary as a wild ex-con. If everyone sounds the same, you lose that layer of personality that makes dialogue feel alive. You can ask ChatGPT, "Write lines for a cynical ex-cop and an idealistic rookie arguing over what to do next," and it'll give each voice a different flavor. Use that to develop consistent tone and cadence for your cast.

And let's not forget the power of silence. Not every line needs a response. Sometimes a look, a pause, or an unfinished sentence says more than words ever could. If you're writing a high-stakes scene, resist the urge to have everyone explain themselves. Let tension build in what's *not* said. Ask ChatGPT to help build those beats. "Write a conversation full of subtext between two characters hiding their true intentions," and you'll get lines dripping with double meanings and half-truths.

Humor also goes a long way in action-adventure dialogue. It humanizes the danger. It relieves the tension. And it makes characters easier to root for. You don't need punchlines every minute, but a well-timed bit of sarcasm or absurdity can lift the mood of a heavy scene. ChatGPT is great for this too. Ask, "Write five funny comebacks a hero could say after surviving a deadly trap," and suddenly your character has charm, not just courage.

When you're working fast, dialogue becomes one of your most efficient tools. You can establish relationships in a page. You can reveal backstory in a single bitter exchange. You can set the next action scene in motion with just a few urgent words. Dialogue isn't a break between action—it *is* action. And when you use it right, it's what readers and viewers remember long after the dust settles.

So whether you're writing a barroom confrontation, a late-night campfire confession, or a frantic radio exchange as the plane nosedives—make those words count. Let them snap. Let them move. Let them reveal.

And with ChatGPT in your corner, feeding you lines, rhythms, conflicts, and secrets—you'll never run out of things for your characters to say. You just need to listen. Then let them speak.

Planning the Escalation: Raising the Stakes

If there's one thing an action-adventure story can never afford to do, it's coast. Once the story starts, it has to keep climbing. Every chapter, every scene, every moment needs to raise the stakes just a little more—or a lot more. That's what gives the story its heartbeat. That's what keeps readers or viewers glued, needing to know what happens next. Escalation isn't just about louder explosions or bigger baddies. It's about deepening the conflict, closing the gap between the hero and disaster, and making every choice harder to walk away from. And when you're writing your story in one day, planning your escalation with intention gives you a clear, focused path forward.

Escalation doesn't mean constant action. It means rising tension. Maybe the first few scenes involve chasing shadows, and then suddenly a body turns up. Maybe your hero is just trying to survive, and then they realize someone they love is in danger. Maybe they thought they had a few allies—until one of them sells them out. Each step forward should shift the balance in some way. What felt like a problem becomes a threat. What felt like a mission becomes personal. What felt like a game turns into life and death.

Start by thinking of your plot in waves. You're not climbing one straight hill—you're going up, then down, then up higher, then down again—but each time the stakes are higher. The goal isn't to exhaust your audience. It's to keep building momentum. The first escape should be tough. The second one should be nearly impossible. The third should cost the hero something. That's how you raise the stakes without losing emotional impact.

This is where ChatGPT really becomes a pressure-cooker. You can ask, "What are five ways to raise the stakes in a jungle-based action-adventure?" and you'll get a buffet of plot escalators. A rival team shows up. The map is stolen. The guide betrays them. A deadly storm traps them in a ravine. Each of these turns doesn't just add noise—they add *problems.* Real obstacles. Emotional tension. New consequences.

Another great move is to shift what the audience thought the story was about. If your hero starts by searching for a lost artifact, halfway through you could reveal that the artifact is part of a larger conspiracy, or a weapon, or a trap set by the villain. Ask ChatGPT, "How can I escalate a treasure hunt into a global threat?" and you'll get ideas that widen the scope of your story while pulling your hero deeper into the fire.

You can also use character relationships to escalate. Maybe the hero's ally is captured. Maybe the villain is someone they once trusted. Maybe their past is catching up with them just when they thought they'd moved on. Ask ChatGPT, "How can my protagonist's personal life collide with the mission?" and suddenly you're not just dealing with external danger—you've got emotional chaos too.

Escalation also works when plans fall apart. Let your characters think they're winning for a moment. Give them a small victory. Then pull the rug. Let ChatGPT help twist the knife: "What's a good twist to ruin my hero's best-laid plan?" Maybe the person they just saved betrays them. Maybe the villain anticipated their move. Maybe help arrives—but it's from someone they can't trust. These turns keep the story tense and unpredictable.

Keep in mind that escalation can be subtle too. It's not always fireballs and chopper crashes. Sometimes it's a slow realization that something is deeply wrong. Sometimes it's doubt creeping into the team. Sometimes it's a moment of hesitation that costs someone their life. Ask ChatGPT to explore emotional stakes with, "How can I increase tension without adding physical danger?" and you'll get rich, quiet moments that cut just as deep as a car chase.

One of the best ways to escalate is to limit time, resources, or options. The hero's gear fails. The villain moves up the timeline. A safe route is blocked. The clock is ticking faster now. Every new obstacle should shrink the hero's window of success. Ask ChatGPT, "How can I build a ticking-clock scenario in the second act?" and you'll be off and running with clear structure.

Think about what the hero stands to lose. Not just their life, but their purpose, their reputation, their people, their soul. As you escalate the story, make those things more vulnerable. The best action-adventure stories don't just destroy cities—they break people open. They force the hero to sacrifice something, or take a risk they've been avoiding since page one. Ask ChatGPT, "What's the worst thing my hero could be forced to do to complete their mission?" and use that answer to turn up the pressure.

Also, let escalation affect the villain. They should be reacting too. Maybe they underestimated the hero. Maybe they're losing control. Maybe they double down and take things to a darker level. Let the escalation play both ways. Ask ChatGPT for help here: "How can my villain respond to a major setback with something even worse?" That counter-escalation keeps the conflict alive and deadly.

As you escalate, pay attention to pacing. You don't want the second act to be a blur of disconnected chaos. Each escalation should feel like a natural consequence of what came before. If you need help keeping it tight, ask ChatGPT, "Give me a sequence of escalating events in an action-adventure story, each raising the stakes and leading to a final confrontation." You'll get a narrative spine that you can then wrap your story around.

By the time you reach the final act, the stakes should be undeniable. Not just big—but personal. Not just loud—but earned. And if you've planned your escalation right, getting there will feel like being dragged uphill by a rope made of adrenaline, emotion, and consequence.

So don't just think about what happens next. Think about what gets *worse*. What gets *heavier*. What gets *harder to walk away from*. That's how you write an action-adventure story that doesn't just explode—it builds. Scene by scene, problem by problem, choice by choice—until there's nowhere left to go but straight into the storm.

Keeping the Pacing Fast and Focused

Pacing is the bloodstream of your action-adventure story. It's what keeps the heart of the reader or viewer pumping, breath held, eyes racing from sentence to sentence or frame to frame. If your story drags, your audience drifts. If it gets too hectic without emotional weight, they disconnect. The sweet spot is somewhere between breakneck and deliberate—fast enough to thrill, focused enough to mean something. And when you're writing a complete story in a single day, mastering pacing isn't just important—it's how you stay in control of the ride.

Action-adventure is built on movement, tension, momentum. It's not just about explosions—it's about forward motion. Something should always be happening: a chase, a discovery, a betrayal, a reveal, a plan gone wrong. But none of that matters if it's just noise. Fast pacing without focus is like a rollercoaster with no track—it's chaos that doesn't go anywhere. You need each scene to drive the story, develop the characters, and lead to something bigger.

So how do you do that? Start by thinking in beats. What needs to happen in this scene that moves the story forward? Is it a clue being uncovered? A decision being made? An enemy getting closer? If a scene isn't doing at least one of those things, cut it or condense it. That's where ChatGPT can help you think clearly. You can ask, "What's the story function of this scene?" or "How can I tighten this chapter to keep the momentum going?" and you'll get suggestions that cut fluff and sharpen purpose.

One of the best techniques to control pacing is to enter scenes late and leave early. You don't need to show your character walking into the building, ordering a coffee, checking their watch, and then finally getting the secret message. Drop us in when the message slides across the table. End the scene when the character realizes what it means. Start at the moment of impact, and then move on. You can use ChatGPT to reframe long sequences: "Rewrite this scene starting with the moment the character is ambushed," and suddenly you've shaved minutes and added tension.

Dialogue is another pacing tool. Shorter exchanges, faster back-and-forths, clipped responses—all of it builds rhythm. When the scene needs to move fast, your dialogue should match. Ask ChatGPT, "Rewrite this conversation to feel tense and urgent," and you'll get lines that cut to the bone. But don't make every scene frantic. The contrast between high-speed and stillness is what makes the fast parts really hit.

Description also plays a huge role in pacing. In an action scene, you want to limit internal monologue and lengthy exposition. Use sharp sensory details—movement, sound, flashes of visual info. You're painting the scene with a speed brush. If you describe every piece of furniture in a burning room, the fire loses its power. Ask ChatGPT for help with tightening: "Condense this paragraph while keeping the sense of danger," and watch your scene go from bulky to bulletproof.

Another smart move is to constantly push toward urgency. A good action-adventure story always feels like the clock is ticking. There's no time to waste. Every delay costs something. Whether it's an actual timer on a bomb, or a race to stop the villain, or a personal deadline like saving someone before it's too late—your story should always feel like something is slipping away. You can even structure your whole story around time pressure. Ask ChatGPT, "How can I build a ticking clock into this mission?" and you'll be handed devices that push your characters harder and keep the audience hooked.

Transitions matter too. The space between scenes is often where pacing drags. Instead of letting things cool down too much, create tension between chapters. End scenes on cliffhangers, questions, reveals, or decisions. Something that demands the next scene immediately. Don't resolve everything neatly—let the story bleed forward. If you're struggling with transitions, ChatGPT can help: "Write a cliffhanger line to end this chapter on suspense," and suddenly you've got a reason to keep writing.

One of the biggest pacing mistakes writers make is over-explaining. Action-adventure readers don't need to be spoon-fed. Trust them to pick up context. Trust your characters to speak through action. If something isn't essential to the current moment or the emotional journey, trim it. Don't tell us what the character is about to do—just let them do it. Ask ChatGPT, "Simplify this exposition so it doesn't slow the pace," and you'll get cleaner, faster narrative flow.

Another tip: vary the rhythm. Not every scene needs to be high-energy. In fact, if everything is turned up to eleven, it all starts to feel the same. Your pacing should have highs and lows—moments to breathe, to reflect, to connect. A quiet scene between two characters can give the next explosion more weight. But even those slower moments should serve the story. Ask ChatGPT, "How can I make this quiet scene still feel urgent or emotionally charged?" and you'll strike the balance between calm and tension.

When you're writing fast—as in one-day-speed fast—your pacing habits matter even more. It's easy to wander off course or lose steam in the middle. That's why having pacing checkpoints can help. Ask yourself at the end of each scene: Did something change? Did someone learn something, lose something, choose something? If the answer is no, you've hit a speed bump. Ask ChatGPT to help smooth the pacing: "What could happen in this scene to raise the stakes or complicate the mission?"

And don't forget the emotional pacing. Action is one thing—but emotion is what keeps people locked in. Escalating danger should also escalate feeling. Make the hero feel more vulnerable, more determined, more conflicted with each obstacle. Ask ChatGPT, "How can I mirror the plot pacing with an emotional arc?" and suddenly you're writing a story that's not just fast, but deep.

Pacing isn't about writing faster—it's about writing sharper. Making every line matter. Every scene count. Every chapter drive the story forward with clarity, pressure, and purpose. And when you're working in tandem with ChatGPT, you'll never be stuck staring at a slow spot again. You'll always have a way to tighten, tweak, or turbo-charge your scenes in seconds.

So keep the engine running. Keep the tension alive. Let your pacing be the force that propels your story like a missile through obstacle after obstacle, right to the final explosion. Fast. Focused. Relentless. That's how you keep your reader or viewer turning pages long after they meant to stop.

Making Action Scenes Leap off the Page

Action scenes are the lifeblood of an action-adventure story. They're what audiences come for, what they remember, and what makes your story feel like it's got real momentum. But writing action isn't just about chaos. It's not about listing who punches who or how many things explode. Great action scenes aren't just loud—they're cinematic. They're clean. They're emotional. And they make the reader *feel* like they're inside the moment, not just watching from the outside. If you're going to make your action scenes leap off the page, you need clarity, rhythm, stakes, and character driving every single move.

When you're writing fast—like one full story in a single day—action scenes can easily become either rushed or overwritten. That's where ChatGPT becomes your best sparring partner. It can help you sketch, choreograph, tighten, and punch up your scenes on demand. But the real trick is understanding how to structure action for the page. And that starts with *intent.*

Every action scene should exist for a reason. It's not just there to look cool. It's there to reveal something. Maybe the hero proves they're not ready yet. Maybe they discover a hidden strength. Maybe they lose something important, or someone close. The worst thing an action scene can do is leave the characters in the exact same place they were before it happened. The moment the dust clears, *something* should be different. You can ask ChatGPT, "What could change emotionally for my hero during this fight?" and you'll get angles that make the action matter.

Next comes clarity. You want your reader to see what's happening. Not sort of see it—*really* see it. One of the fastest ways to kill an action scene is to make it confusing. Who's doing what? Where are they standing? What just happened? You want the geography of the moment to be clear, even in motion. Describe space, movement, and sequence with precision. You don't need to describe every punch, but you do need to keep the reader oriented. You can use ChatGPT to help outline the scene before you write it. Say, "Describe a fight scene on a narrow rooftop with a slippery surface," and you'll get a beat-by-beat list you can shape into your own voice.

Pacing is key. Action scenes are not the place for long, winding sentences. They're about rhythm. Shorter lines, quick reactions, tight descriptions. If the characters are in a frantic chase, the sentences should reflect that. If they're in a brutal, methodical brawl, the writing should feel heavier, more deliberate. You can ask ChatGPT to rewrite your scene with a different pace: "Make this hand-to-hand combat scene more fast and frantic," or, "Slow this down for a tense, brutal fight." It will help you adjust the tempo to match the tone.

Then there's sensory detail. Don't just write what the characters do—write what they *feel.* The heat of the engine room. The sting of sweat in the eyes. The scrape of concrete against knuckles. The silence just before the ambush. These little touches are what bring action to life. You can ask ChatGPT, "Give me sensory details for a chase through a crowded market," and suddenly you've got scents, sounds, textures—all those things that pull the reader inside the scene.

What separates a decent action scene from a great one is emotion. You want more than adrenaline—you want consequence. Your hero shouldn't just be ducking bullets—they should be making decisions under pressure. Action reveals character. Does your hero save someone else or themselves? Do they hesitate? Do they take a risk they wouldn't have before? These are the moments that show us who they really are. ChatGPT can help layer this in. Ask, "What internal conflict could the hero experience during this rescue mission?" and you'll get insight that deepens the impact.

Choreography is another element you don't want to overlook. You can absolutely block out your scene like a movie director. Who's coming from where? What's in the environment they can use? Is there a window to jump through, a loose pipe to swing from, a weapon to improvise with? The environment can turn a basic brawl into something unforgettable. Ask ChatGPT to help brainstorm: "Give me ten ways to use a museum setting in a fight scene," and suddenly the exhibit becomes the weapon.

Action scenes also benefit from escalation. You don't want the energy to plateau. Start with a problem, then make it worse. Maybe the hero is cornered. Then the villain arrives. Then the building starts to collapse. Each beat should raise the tension and reduce the character's options. You can ask ChatGPT, "How can I escalate a fight scene in an abandoned train station?" and you'll get levels of chaos that build naturally and drive the tension forward.

Another way to make your action scenes jump off the page is to play with contrast. Big moments hit harder after quiet ones. Silence makes the explosion louder. A character whispering before pulling the trigger lands harder than a scream. Think about pacing within the scene, not just in the structure of the story. Ask ChatGPT, "What's a good moment of quiet tension to drop into this gunfight?" and you might find your scene becomes more cinematic, more alive.

Don't forget the aftermath. Action scenes aren't over when the last punch is thrown. They linger. Characters might limp away, patch themselves up, argue about what went wrong, or take a moment to reflect. That cool-down moment is where emotion catches up with adrenaline. It's where readers breathe—and where your characters deepen. Ask ChatGPT, "Write a post-action beat where the hero realizes what the fight cost them," and you'll anchor your scene in something meaningful.

When writing fast, it helps to sketch your scene with broad strokes first. Where does it take place? What's the obstacle? Who's involved? What's the goal? What's the twist? You can use ChatGPT to map this out with a single prompt. Say, "Outline a three-phase chase scene through an airport ending on the tarmac," and you'll have a clear structure to write from in minutes.

In the end, action scenes leap off the page when they're written with intent, energy, and emotional weight. They're not about how many things explode—they're about who your characters become while everything explodes around them. Let the action reveal, change, and challenge. Use tight language, vivid details, smart choreography, and heart. And let ChatGPT help you shape, reshape, and heighten every beat.

Because when your reader feels like they're in the middle of the chaos—ducking under a collapsing bridge, racing through a crumbling temple, or trading blows on the wing of a plane at 30,000 feet—that's when your action scene isn't just being read. It's being *lived.*

Writing Visual Action for Screen and Prose

Writing action for the screen and writing action for the page are two different beasts—same energy, different delivery. One is built to be seen, the other to be imagined. But in both cases, you're creating something *visual*. Action is a language of movement. It's about bodies in motion, decisions in crisis, cause and effect playing out in physical space. Whether you're writing a novel or a screenplay, the goal is to *show* the reader or the viewer what's happening in a way that's vivid, fast, and emotionally charged.

The good news? The foundation is the same. You're trying to make the audience see what you see. The difference lies in how you translate it.

Let's start with screenwriting. When you write action for the screen, you're writing for production. That means you need to be concise, clear, and highly visual. You're not telling the director or actors what to feel—you're showing them what's physically happening in the scene. Action lines in screenplays are short. Often fragmented. Always visual. You're describing exactly what the camera would see. The rhythm of these sentences often mimics the rhythm of the action itself.

For example:

EXT. DESERT ROAD – DAY

The SUV fishtails across the sand. Bullets ping off the hood. JAX dives out, rolls, comes up with his pistol. Fires once—hits the tire of the pursuing jeep. The jeep flips. Sand and metal in the air.

Each line is a beat of action. Quick, sharp, lean. No internal monologue. No fancy prose. Just action as movement, shot by shot. That's what the camera needs. That's what the actor needs. And you can use ChatGPT to refine this kind of writing quickly. Ask, "Write a fast-paced chase scene in screenplay format," and you'll get a scene that hits all the right beats with clean visual language.

Now, for prose—novels, short stories, and anything meant to be read off the page—you have a little more room to breathe. But not too much. Readers still want to *see* the action, not be told about it. The difference here is that you can dip into the character's experience. You can explore sensations, reactions, thoughts—but you still need to keep the pace moving.

Here's how that same action scene might look in prose:

The SUV skidded sideways, sand spitting in every direction. Gunfire cracked across the dunes—metal clanged as bullets chewed into the hood. Jax dove out the door, hit the ground hard, rolled with the momentum. Pain shot through his ribs. He came up with his pistol, breath tight in his throat. One shot. The trailing jeep's front tire burst. The vehicle lurched, then flipped—rolling end over end in a cloud of dust and flying steel.

Same events. Different texture. In prose, you're still writing *cinematically*, but you're also writing *sensually*. What does it feel like to hit the ground? What sound does the gun make? What flashes through the character's head in that moment of danger? You have the freedom to color the scene with emotional texture, but every sentence should still drive the action forward.

With ChatGPT, you can play with both styles. Ask, "Write this action scene as a novel passage," and then, "Now convert it to screenplay format." This back-and-forth teaches you how to think in both languages—and how to keep the storytelling fluid regardless of the format.

When you're working fast—say, writing an entire action-adventure story in one day—you might not have time to finesse every sentence, but you *do* have time to make your action scenes visual. Whether you're writing for screen or prose, keep asking: Can I *see* this? Can I *feel* this? Am I moving the story or just decorating it?

A good trick in either format is to zoom in and zoom out. Start wide—what's the setting, what's happening, what's the chaos. Then zoom in—what's the hero doing, what are they feeling, how are they reacting. Then zoom back out for the impact. For example:

Wide: The temple exploded behind them, stone and fire tearing into the sky.

Close: Rey's lungs burned as she ran. Her hands stung with cuts from the shattered tablet. She didn't look back.

Impact: The sound reached them seconds later—like the earth splitting open.

That rhythm works for both formats. For screenplays, break it into beats. For prose, give it the texture of thought and sensation. You can use ChatGPT to build this rhythm into scenes. Ask, "Write an action scene with a wide-close-wide camera feel," and you'll get that cinematic layering.

One major pitfall in both screen and prose action writing is over-description. You don't need to choreograph every move. Just the essential ones. A fight scene where you describe every jab, dodge, and parry becomes mechanical. Instead, focus on the *turning points*. The reversal. The moment the hero almost loses. The moment they take control. Let ChatGPT help you identify those moments: "What are the key beats in a one-on-one sword fight in a collapsing tower?" and build your scene around that skeleton.

Use the environment too. Action is always better when characters interact with their surroundings. In a marketplace chase, are they ducking under vendor stalls? Flipping tables? Using objects as weapons? The more grounded the action is in place, the more real it feels. Ask ChatGPT for specifics: "Give me five creative ways to use a hotel setting in an action sequence." Each idea becomes a beat you can plug directly into your scene.

And finally, remember that emotion is action. A punch is just a punch unless it means something. If the hero's throwing that punch because they've been betrayed, or they're trying to save someone, or they've finally snapped—*that's* what makes the scene leap off the page. The action should always be the physical result of a deeper tension.

So, write with your eyes. Think like a director when you're writing prose. Think like a poet when you're writing screenplays. Let ChatGPT help you build rhythm, structure, sensory texture, and physical beats. Your scenes don't need to be big to be thrilling. They just need to be visual, purposeful, and charged with story.

Because when action scenes leap off the page, they're not just cool—they're unforgettable.

Bringing Emotion into Explosions

Explosions are easy. Emotion is hard. But the best action-adventure stories? They do both—at the same time. An explosion by itself is just noise, fire, and debris. But an explosion that tears apart a relationship, a dream, or a secret—that's storytelling. That's where the audience sits up, leans in, and *feels* something deeper than the blast. So when you're writing your fast-paced, high-stakes story, don't think of action and emotion as two separate tracks. Think of them as twin engines. And when you fire both at once, your story takes off like nothing else.

It's easy to get caught up in the visual side of action—blazing vehicles, crumbling towers, machine gun fire in the rain—but if your characters aren't invested, the audience won't be either. And if you're writing this story in one day, it's even more important to make every big moment count. You don't have time for filler. You need to make every punch land both physically *and* emotionally.

So how do you bring emotion into your action scenes? You start by asking, "What does this explosion *mean* to the character?" Not just what happens, but why it matters. Is this a mission they were warned not to take? A place they thought was safe? A final betrayal? Maybe the explosion represents a loss of control, or the death of a belief, or the climax of years of guilt and denial. Even if it's just a building going up, you've got to anchor that destruction to something personal.

Let's say your hero watches the safehouse explode—maybe they were supposed to protect it. Maybe someone they care about was inside. Maybe the villain knew exactly how to twist the knife. That's not just spectacle. That's heartbreak. That's fuel. You can use ChatGPT to help develop these connections. Ask, "How can this explosion deepen the emotional arc of my character?" or "What personal stakes could be tied to a mission gone wrong?"

Another way to inject emotion is through internal conflict *during* the chaos. Think about what's going through the character's mind as they run from the blast, as they fall from the chopper, as they fire back under pressure. Are they second-guessing themselves? Reliving a past trauma? Fighting to keep calm for someone else's sake? This inner world adds a pulse beneath the noise. Ask ChatGPT to layer this in: "Write an action scene where the hero is haunted by a past failure while fighting for their life." Suddenly your action scene has depth, not just velocity.

Dialogue in action is also a killer opportunity to hit both notes at once. A desperate shout, a quiet promise, a final goodbye over a radio before it cuts to static—those lines can become the emotional glue of the scene. Keep them short. Keep them raw. And use them to underline the *why* behind the action. Ask ChatGPT, "Give me emotional dialogue to drop into a high-stakes escape sequence," and you'll get lines that add punch to the punches.

Relationships, too, are key. Explosions matter more when someone else is involved. Maybe your hero's trying to save their sibling, their team, their old mentor. Maybe they fail. Maybe they barely succeed, and the cost is written across their face. You can design your action scenes around emotional beats between characters. Ask ChatGPT, "What's a great emotional beat between two characters during a gunfight?" and you'll get ideas that keep the humanity front and center.

Don't forget guilt, either. Guilt is a powerful emotion in action-adventure. Your hero might *win* the fight but feel like they lost something more important. Innocents died. A promise was broken. A villain was allowed to escape. These aren't just plot points—they're emotional landmines. Use them. After a chaotic moment, give your hero a second to feel it. Even if they have to keep moving, that flicker of emotion makes the audience lean in. Ask ChatGPT, "Write a short inner monologue of a hero who just caused collateral damage," and that single paragraph might be what makes the scene stick.

Let's talk sacrifice. Explosions are often used as the climax of a sacrificial moment. Someone stays behind to hold off the enemy. Someone throws themselves over a detonator. If you build up to it right, those scenes hit *hard*. But the key is in the *build-up*. The character has to mean something to someone. There has to be an unresolved tension, a promise, a history. You don't need ten chapters to create that, either—you just need clarity and heart. Ask ChatGPT, "Write a scene where a reluctant teammate sacrifices themselves for someone they used to hate," and you'll see how fast an emotional arc can bloom in the middle of chaos.

Another approach is to make explosions symbolic. Let the destruction represent something more than just danger. Maybe it's the end of the hero's innocence. The destruction of a home that can't be rebuilt. The moment a mentor's lies are exposed. When the fire clears, the character isn't just in a new location—they're in a new headspace. That's how you write a transformation, not just a detonation. Ask ChatGPT, "How can a physical explosion represent a psychological turning point for my character?" and you'll open up a world of meaning beneath the spectacle.

Even villains can add emotion to the explosion. Maybe the antagonist is someone your hero once trusted. Maybe the bomb is planted in a place that means something. Maybe the villain gives your hero a choice—save the girl, or stop the weapon. The more complex the conflict, the more powerful the action becomes. Ask ChatGPT, "What's a way to create an emotional dilemma during an action climax?" and you'll get options that hit all the right nerves.

At the end of the day, it's not the explosion itself that makes the audience gasp—it's the *cost* of the explosion. What's lost. What's realized. What's changed. You're not just blowing up a bridge—you're burning a path, lighting a fuse, ripping through something emotional that can't be undone.

So write big. Write bold. But write from the heart, even when the grenades are flying. Let ChatGPT help you sharpen every beat, find every emotional crack, and build action scenes that shake your characters as much as the reader. That's how you make explosions more than just fire and noise.

That's how you make them *matter*.

Weaving a Theme through the Chaos

Action-adventure stories are famous for spectacle—chases, explosions, impossible escapes, and high-stakes showdowns. But what separates a good action-adventure from a *great* one is the thread that holds all the chaos together: the theme. It's the invisible spine of the story. The idea beneath the action. The question your story is asking over and over again in different ways. You don't have to shout it. You don't have to explain it. You just have to *weave it in*—line by line, scene by scene—so that when the final dust settles, the audience realizes the story wasn't just exciting. It *meant* something.

Themes don't slow a story down. They give it resonance. Think about *Die Hard*—sure, it's about terrorists and skyscrapers, but underneath all the glass and gunfire, it's a story about reconnection, about a broken marriage and a man trying to fix something while bullets fly. Or *Indiana Jones and the Last Crusade*—beneath the ancient relics and Nazi punch-outs, it's a story about a son who finally gets to understand his father. The action serves the theme. And because it does, it hits harder.

So how do you find your theme—and how do you keep it alive while the world's falling apart around your hero?

Start by asking: What is my story *really* about?

Maybe it's about redemption. Trust. Sacrifice. Identity. Justice. Maybe your hero starts out believing something false—like that people can't be trusted, or that power is the only protection—and through the chaos, they learn something deeper. The plot is the fire. The theme is what burns away the lies. And ChatGPT is your co-pilot in figuring this out. You can say, "Suggest a central theme for an action-adventure story about a rogue spy and a secret child," and suddenly you've got threads of family, trust, legacy to work with.

Once you know your theme, you weave it through your characters. Not just your hero—the whole cast. Maybe your hero believes in justice, but the sidekick is all about survival. Maybe the villain is a twisted version of the same ideal. That's when your scenes start reflecting your theme in every direction. Ask ChatGPT, "Create character dynamics that explore the theme of redemption," and you'll get relationships built to test, reinforce, or challenge your core idea.

Next, bring that theme into the world and the action. If your story's about control vs. chaos, set it in a place that's breaking down—a city in riot, a collapsing regime, a storm-ravaged landscape. Let the environment reflect the internal struggle. If your story's about sacrifice, let your action scenes be filled with impossible choices. Save one person or another. Risk everything or live with the guilt. The explosions and set-pieces aren't random—they're shaped to keep your theme alive. Ask ChatGPT, "What are action scenes that reflect the theme of loyalty vs. betrayal?" and you'll get ideas where the emotional and the physical are on the same track.

Dialogue is another place to echo your theme—but lightly. You don't need speeches. Just a few lines that give us a window into what the characters believe. A moment of doubt. A question thrown in the middle of a firefight. A comment made in jest that cuts a little too close. Let the characters speak their beliefs—and then let the story challenge them. You can ask ChatGPT, "Give me five short lines of dialogue that reflect a character's fear of becoming like their enemy," and you'll get emotional material that fits right inside your action without slowing it down.

Here's the magic part: theme doesn't have to be obvious at first. In fact, it shouldn't be. Let it rise like smoke. Let the audience *feel* it before they *see* it. A good theme leaves echoes. By the time your hero reaches the final showdown, they're not just fighting the villain—they're standing at the crossroads of the story's biggest question. Do they change? Do they break the cycle? Do they fall into the same trap? This is where theme and climax collide. And that's where you get stories that hit the heart, not just the nerves.

You can also plant your theme visually. If your story's about identity, maybe there's a motif of mirrors, masks, or name changes. If it's about power, maybe there's a recurring object—like a weapon or a relic—that characters project their beliefs onto. Use ChatGPT to help plant these threads. Ask, "What are visual symbols that support a theme of freedom vs. control?" and you'll get images you can sprinkle throughout your story for that extra layer of meaning.

Even your story structure can reflect your theme. If the story is about second chances, let the midpoint be a failed attempt. If it's about sacrifice, let the rising action be full of selfish choices until the hero finally chooses someone else over themselves. Let your plot arc be the *proof* of the theme. Ask ChatGPT, "How can my story structure mirror a character's journey from fear to courage?" and it'll help you design scenes that grow naturally from that idea.

And don't worry if you don't figure out the theme before you start writing. Sometimes it shows up halfway through. Sometimes you see it clearly only at the end. The beauty of using a tool like ChatGPT is that you can spot the theme once it surfaces, then go back and thread it through earlier scenes. Ask, "How can I reinforce the theme of identity in this early scene?" and suddenly everything starts to connect.

A great theme doesn't sit above the action. It runs under it. It's the quiet pulse beneath the chaos. It's the reason the audience remembers your story long after the last explosion fades. So keep the thrills, keep the chases, keep the cliffhangers—but give them meaning.

Let every choice, every blow, every turning point be a step toward answering your story's biggest question. And when that question is finally answered, in a whisper or a war cry—that's when your action-adventure stops being just fun...

And becomes unforgettable.

Action in Exotic Places: Making Settings Work

There's something undeniably thrilling about action-adventure stories that take place in exotic, far-flung locations. Whether it's a dusty Moroccan bazaar, a frozen military outpost in Siberia, an abandoned temple deep in the Amazon, or a neon-soaked street market in Bangkok, these backdrops aren't just eye candy—they're fuel. Great settings aren't passive—they shape the story, create obstacles, provide inspiration for action, and leave a taste in the reader's imagination that lingers long after the final explosion.

The location in an action-adventure story should feel like a character in its own right. It should breathe, shift, and respond to what's happening around it. When you drop your hero into a new place, you're not just changing the view. You're changing the rules. That's what makes exotic settings so powerful—they offer unfamiliar terrain, cultural nuance, unpredictable elements, and natural environmental hazards that can all be used to amplify your action.

So how do you write these locations in a way that feels alive, urgent, and essential to the story?

The first rule is this: *let the setting affect the action.* Don't just drop a fight scene into a jungle because it looks cool—make the jungle matter. Mud, humidity, low visibility, bugs in the eyes, vines catching on boots, weapons jamming from moisture—let it shape the scene. If the setting could be replaced with a hotel lobby and the action still plays the same, you haven't used the location yet. Ask ChatGPT, "How can I make a jungle setting affect a chase scene?" and you'll instantly get textures and hazards that change the rhythm of the moment.

Great exotic settings also challenge the characters. Maybe your protagonist doesn't speak the language. Maybe they're unfamiliar with the customs. Maybe the altitude makes them weak, or the terrain forces them to change tactics. This kind of discomfort creates tension, mistakes, and improvisation—all of which make for better scenes. You can tell ChatGPT, "Give me five location-based obstacles in a Himalayan village," and suddenly your action scene isn't just a shootout—it's a test of endurance and adaptability.

Another advantage of exotic locations is the opportunity to use architecture and history in your action. A fight on the roof of a floating pagoda. A chase through underground tunnels beneath an old Roman coliseum. A standoff in a war-scarred cathedral where bullets ricochet off stone columns carved centuries ago. You're layering time, space, and character all at once. Ask ChatGPT to generate options like, "List unique action set-pieces in an ancient mountain monastery," and you'll get ideas you wouldn't think of on your own.

Exotic doesn't have to mean remote, either. A street market in Nairobi, a coastal city in Croatia, a cave system in Vietnam—these are places people live and breathe, full of color and culture, danger and beauty. Use the people, the customs, the sounds and smells of these places to inject vibrancy into your scenes. You can ask ChatGPT, "Describe a tense dialogue scene set in a crowded night bazaar in Istanbul," and you'll get a scene laced with atmosphere that crackles with energy.

Pacing and structure can also be affected by location. If your story takes place in the Arctic, scenes will be shorter, faster—your characters can't survive out in the cold for long. If it's in the desert, exhaustion, thirst, and heat become obstacles. If it's on a tropical island, travel may be slow, but the isolation raises the stakes. Let the location change the rules of engagement. Ask ChatGPT, "What time-sensitive challenges could happen during a jungle expedition?" and you'll get instant tension built into the setting itself.

Visuals matter too. Readers of action-adventure want to *see* where they are. But you don't need pages of description. A few well-placed details can do the trick. The color of the sky, the texture of the ground, the hum of wildlife, the smell of incense or decay. These small touches create a strong sense of place. You can ask ChatGPT, "Describe the atmosphere of an abandoned island temple at night," and you'll get a sensory palette you can weave into your scene as you write.

Using location also allows for improvised tools, weapons, and cover. A banana cart becomes a barricade. A ceremonial spear becomes a lifesaving weapon. A festival crowd becomes both shield and chaos. When the characters are forced to use what's around them, the action feels more inventive and grounded. Ask ChatGPT, "Give me ideas for how a hero could use a market setting during a shootout," and you'll be surprised how many scene beats you can build from that single location.

Emotionally, exotic settings can trigger internal shifts too. Maybe the hero visited the place once as a child. Maybe they're confronting a past trauma in the ruins of a city where it happened. Maybe they're reminded of what they've lost, or what they still hope to find. Even amid danger, an exotic location can offer moments of awe, reflection, or fear. Ask ChatGPT, "Write a reflective moment for a character seeing a war-torn city they once called home," and you can balance action with emotional gravity.

If you're writing a story quickly—as in, one epic adventure in a single day—having your exotic settings pre-planned can save you a lot of time. You can ask ChatGPT early in the writing day, "Give me a list of exotic locations that could each serve as a chapter setting," and use that as your map. Each place becomes a new challenge. A new flavor. A new chance to bring a different kind of fire to the story.

Remember, the setting isn't just where the action takes place—it *is* part of the action. Use it. Play with it. Make it impossible to separate your story from the place it happens. When a reader or viewer says, "That scene *had* to happen there," you've done your job right.

So go exotic. Go wild. Drop your hero in the snow, the sand, the steam, the salt, the jungle, the skyline, the wreckage. Let the world challenge them, shape them, and change the story one location at a time.

Because when your setting works *with* the story, not just in it, that's when your action-adventure becomes a full-body experience. One where the reader's not just watching...

They're *there.*

From Map to Mayhem: Writing Globe-Trotting Stories

There's something timeless and irresistible about a globe-trotting action-adventure story. The moment your hero boards a plane, train, or rusted-out jeep to race across continents in pursuit of a treasure, truth, or villain, you're tapping into a narrative style that spans from *Indiana Jones* to *Mission: Impossible* to *Uncharted*. It's escapism with momentum. Discovery wrapped in danger. And when done right, the reader or viewer doesn't just follow the hero—they feel like they've packed their bags, stamped their passport, and thrown themselves into the chaos right alongside them.

Writing a globe-trotting adventure doesn't mean simply picking a bunch of cool places and stitching them together. You're not just placing pins in a map—you're building a path, a chase, a journey that escalates with each stop. The locations must feel earned, connected, and meaningful. When the story moves, it should do more than change the scenery. It should raise the stakes.

If you're writing your entire story in one day, this kind of narrative has a built-in advantage: it creates structure. You move from Point A to B to C, and each new setting acts as a new "level" in your adventure. Ask ChatGPT, "Give me a series of global locations that build tension and variety for an action-adventure plot," and you'll get an instant world tour complete with tone shifts. Maybe it starts in Cairo, moves to a rainy Paris street, then to an underwater cave system in the Philippines. That's not just travel—it's narrative movement.

When plotting a globe-trotting story, you want every location to offer something unique. It could be an environmental challenge (thin air in the Himalayas), a cultural element (a ritual in Papua New Guinea), a piece of history (ancient Roman catacombs), or a resource the hero needs (a hacker hiding in Tokyo). Don't let your locations blur together. Give each one a personality. Ask ChatGPT, "Describe the tone and visual style of a scene set in an abandoned Icelandic fishing village," and you'll get instant texture you can plug straight into your narrative.

One of the key tricks to making globe-trotting stories work is to build narrative propulsion between the locations. Don't just jump for the sake of it—make each destination the result of discovery, consequence, or desperation. The hero uncovers a clue in one city that points to the next. They flee from danger in one country straight into a trap in another. The villain's path crisscrosses the globe, and the hero stays just one step behind—or ahead. You can structure this quickly by asking ChatGPT, "Create a chain of locations linked by clues in a treasure hunt-style adventure," and you'll have a reason to move that's tied directly to your plot.

Transportation becomes part of the tension. The flight that gets hijacked. The freighter with a smuggled artifact onboard. The train where everyone's a suspect. The motorcycle chase across cobblestone rooftops. Don't skip the in-between moments—they're not just transitions, they're action opportunities. You can turn travel itself into a battleground. Ask ChatGPT, "What are five action set-pieces that take place during travel between global destinations?" and you'll get options that turn downtime into drama.

Another huge advantage of globe-trotting stories is contrast. A dusty archaeological dig followed by a neon-lit cybercrime den in Seoul. A snowstorm siege in Siberia cut by a sweaty jungle rescue in Colombia. These shifts in setting keep your story visually and emotionally fresh. Use them to show how your characters adapt—or fall apart—under changing circumstances. Ask ChatGPT, "What emotional changes might a character go through as they travel from a familiar home to hostile terrain?" and you'll start building a psychological journey to match the physical one.

You can also use the global scope to show different factions, allies, and enemies. In one country, your hero is protected. In another, they're hunted. A friend in Berlin turns out to be a spy. A taxi driver in Cairo becomes an unexpected ally.

You're creating a web of relationships that stretch across borders. Ask ChatGPT to help you build this out: "Give me five international allies with unique backgrounds and motives for helping the hero," and your globe-spanning cast comes to life.

Maps can also play a literal role. Have your characters track their progress with a hand-drawn map, or a digital interface slowly filling with red pins. Let the audience see the journey. The growing complexity. The narrowing odds. Even something as simple as a red thread connecting cities on a wall of photographs can make the journey feel tactile. Ask ChatGPT, "How can I use maps visually in a story to enhance tension and progress?" and it'll give you more than just lines and locations—it'll give you storytelling tools.

Now, there's one thing to watch out for: don't just use exotic settings as flavor. Respect the cultures and locations you're writing about. Even if the story moves fast, take time to make the world feel real. If you're writing a scene in Morocco, don't reduce it to "sand and markets." Let the setting be more than decoration. Ask ChatGPT for help: "Describe the sounds, smells, and energy of a sunrise in Marrakesh," and let your characters move through the real textures of the world, not a postcard version.

And remember, globe-trotting doesn't always mean flying around the world. You can write a globe-trotting story in a single city if the neighborhoods, factions, and stakes feel distinct enough. Or across time, if your locations shift through history. The idea is movement, scope, momentum—and the feeling that the story is hurtling toward something big and global in scale.

So plan your route. Pick your cities, jungles, oceans, caves, and fortresses. Make your map messy and full of promise. Let each new location shift the rules, raise the stakes, and change the game.

And when you're ready, let ChatGPT help you turn that map into mayhem. One thrilling, globe-spanning, pulse-pounding scene at a time.

How to Structure a 3-Act Action-Adventure Story

You've got the idea. You've got the characters. You've even got the explosions and chase scenes ready to go. But if you want all those great pieces to click into a story that actually *works*—one that pulls the reader or viewer through from start to finish—you need structure. The three-act structure is the backbone of most successful action-adventure stories, and when used well, it doesn't feel like structure at all. It feels like momentum. It feels like a story with gravity, purpose, and rhythm. When you're writing in a single day, having this framework in your head is like having a compass and a map. It keeps you moving in the right direction.

So let's break it down in the most practical way possible, and keep it loose enough to fit your style but clear enough to give your story shape.

Act One: The Launch Pad

This is the setup. The world, the characters, and the spark that lights the fire. In action-adventure, Act One doesn't have time to meander. You want to grab your reader fast, drop them into motion, and establish the stakes as soon as possible. It usually starts with a cold open or a mini-action scene—something that throws the audience into danger, intrigue, or mystery before the full story kicks in.

Your protagonist is introduced in their status quo—maybe they're already deep in the game, or maybe they're reluctant to get involved. Either way, we need to know what makes them tick. What do they want? What are they trying to escape, recover, protect, or uncover? The inciting incident—a murder, a theft, a betrayal, a mysterious clue—should come quickly and send them on their journey. Something needs to disrupt the ordinary and force a choice.

By the end of Act One, the hero commits. They cross the threshold. They board the plane. They accept the mission. The world changes—and they're not going back.

If you want help fleshing this out quickly, ChatGPT can act as your development partner. Ask, "Help me design Act One of an action-adventure about a rogue archeologist framed for theft," and it'll offer plot beats, turning points, and character motivation in a clear path forward.

Act Two: The Rising Storm

This is the longest section and the meat of your story. The hero is now in the adventure, navigating a series of escalating conflicts, dangerous encounters, and emotional challenges. It's also the act where many writers get lost because it's easy to fill it with action without direction. That's where *rising tension* becomes your friend. Each new scene should either increase the stakes, reveal a new complication, or bring your hero closer to—or farther from—their goal.

In the first half of Act Two, the hero is usually reacting. They're chasing leads, solving problems, trying to survive. They meet allies and enemies. They discover that things are bigger and messier than they thought. This is where your set-pieces belong—your car chases, brawls in ancient temples, your stealth missions gone sideways.

Around the midpoint, something *changes*. A reveal flips the story. Maybe the person they trusted turns out to be the villain. Maybe the object they're chasing is a fake. Maybe the villain wins a round. This moment shifts the direction of the story and usually forces the hero to evolve.

In the second half of Act Two, the hero becomes more active. They stop reacting and start choosing. They begin to lead. They face their flaws. But things still go wrong. And by the end of the act, you hit the *lowest point*. The betrayal lands. The villain gets what they want. The hero is captured, broken, or forced to make a terrible sacrifice. This is the moment the audience thinks it's all over.

ChatGPT is great for structuring this entire act. You can ask, "Give me a midpoint twist for an action-adventure set on a hijacked cargo ship," or, "What are three emotional setbacks my hero could face before the final battle?" and suddenly you've got a second act that drives.

Act Three: The Final Push

This is where your story catches fire. The hero rises from the ashes. They've changed. They see clearly now—about the world, the villain, and themselves. This clarity gives them the strength to act with purpose.

First comes the regroup. A plan is formed, the final push begins, and the last set of obstacles stand in their way. The action is tighter here—focused. The climax should be the biggest, most intense moment of the entire story. Not just in terms of spectacle—but in terms of *emotion*. This is the moment the theme comes full circle. The hero doesn't just fight to win—they fight to *become* who they were meant to be.

Then comes the confrontation. It might be a duel, a heist, a rescue, a ticking clock. It's your job as the writer to make this moment matter. If the villain is a twisted version of your hero, let that conflict come to the surface. If there's something personal at stake, make the final choice cost something.

And once the climax lands, wrap it fast. Don't drag out the ending. Resolve what needs resolving, leave a thread if you're planning a sequel, but let the dust settle while the emotion is still fresh.

If you're unsure about how to stage this, ChatGPT can help here too. Ask, "How can I make my final action scene echo my hero's emotional arc?" or, "What's a climactic setting that reflects a theme of redemption?" and you'll end your story on something meaningful, not just loud.

When you step back, the three-act structure is deceptively simple.

Act One: Set up the world and send the hero into it.

Act Two: Throw them into escalating chaos and make them grow.

Act Three: Let them rise, fight, and finish what they started.

It's a classic for a reason—it works. Especially when you're writing fast and need a solid guidepost.

So build your adventure on this foundation. Use it like scaffolding. Then fill it with characters who bleed, villains who haunt, places that breathe, and action that means something. And with ChatGPT by your side at every act, you'll never run short on ideas, turns, twists, or pacing.

In the end, a great action-adventure isn't just a thrill ride—it's a journey. A transformation. A structured sprint through danger, discovery, and destiny. Just follow the map. Three acts. One hero. A whole world to shake.

The Midpoint Twist That Changes Everything

If the first half of your action-adventure story is a race toward something, then the midpoint twist is the unexpected wall your hero crashes into at full speed. This moment changes everything. It's not a random plot turn—it's a story pivot that deepens the stakes, flips expectations, and forces your characters to see the world, the mission, or themselves in a new light. In fact, a great midpoint twist doesn't just keep the reader or viewer hooked—it redefines what the story is really about.

When you're writing a story in a single day, a midpoint twist becomes a structural anchor. It gives your story a "before" and an "after." The hero might still be chasing the same goal, but now the goal feels heavier, more complicated, or darker than it did when the adventure started. That shift is what creates momentum for Act Two's second half and primes the climax to land with real impact.

So what exactly qualifies as a twist that changes everything?

It's the moment your character learns something that alters their mission. Maybe the artifact they've been chasing is a fake—or worse, it's dangerous. Maybe the villain they've been hunting is actually their mentor. Maybe the government they've been working for is the real enemy. Maybe the innocent person they've been protecting is hiding a secret that could bring down the world. Whatever it is, the twist should raise the emotional stakes while adding urgency and complexity to the physical ones.

The best twists are *earned*. They don't come out of nowhere. You've been laying the groundwork—maybe through a throwaway line, an unexplained reaction, or a background detail that seemed like nothing at the time. Then you pull the thread. Suddenly, the dots connect. The audience has that *"Ohhhh..."* moment. And just like that, they're all-in again.

This is where ChatGPT can be a game-changer for you. If you've written the first half of your story and want help turning it inside out, just say, "Give me a midpoint twist that changes the meaning of everything in this treasure hunt story." Or, "What's a twist that reveals the hero's closest ally is working for the villain?" You'll get scenarios, motivations, and consequences that you can instantly thread into your next few chapters.

Now let's break it down even further. There are a few different *flavors* of midpoint twists that work especially well in action-adventure:

The Revelation Twist

The hero discovers new information that shifts the entire context. The thing they're looking for isn't what they thought. The villain's plan is far more dangerous. The betrayal was never personal—it was systemic. This kind of twist often comes with a clue, a confession, or a flashback that drops the truth like a bomb.

The Betrayal Twist

Someone switches sides. The ally is a mole. The love interest is a spy. The government sends in a cleanup squad. This twist adds emotional weight because it's not just about strategy—it's personal. It leaves the hero stunned, alone, or filled with rage, and that reaction powers the rest of the story. Ask ChatGPT for help with this: "Write a betrayal scene where the hero realizes their guide has been feeding info to the enemy," and you'll get something immediately usable.

The Failure Twist

The mission fails. The bomb goes off. The target escapes. The hero was too late. The world doesn't end, but it changes. This type of twist hits hard because it's about limits. The hero learns that brute strength, clever tricks, or raw determination aren't enough. Something more is needed—something internal.

The Inversion Twist

This is when the story flips. The hunted becomes the hunter. The hero switches sides. The villain saves the hero. The story's moral compass is spun, and suddenly everything feels unfamiliar and risky again. These are the twists that give a story long legs because they introduce a second layer of meaning just as the audience thinks they've figured everything out.

Whatever route you take, a good midpoint twist should do a few key things:

1. **Force a decision.** The hero has to make a new choice, one they weren't expecting to face. Go forward or go home. Break the rules or become part of the problem. Save the world or save one person. The new pressure should hurt.
2. **Change the emotional terrain.** The hero isn't just adjusting the mission—they're adjusting themselves. They're shaken, angry, doubting everything. That vulnerability becomes the emotional thread you carry into Act Three.
3. **Raise the stakes.** If the first half of the story was about stopping a crime, the second half is about stopping a war. If it was about saving someone, now it's about saving *everyone.* The midpoint twist doesn't slow your story down—it launches it harder.

Let's talk technique for a second. How do you *write* this moment?

Start the scene with something familiar. Maybe the hero thinks they're winning. Maybe things are quiet. Let the tension simmer. Then insert a crack. A name they weren't expecting to hear. A face they shouldn't be seeing. A clue that doesn't add up. Let the twist unfold like a trap closing, not a hammer dropping. Let the hero catch up just in time to realize they've already lost something. Use sensory detail—heartbeat, weather, silence—to slow down time and let the moment breathe.

And let the twist echo backward. Make the reader or viewer rethink everything that came before. That moment three chapters ago that didn't make sense? Now it does. That line of dialogue? Now it cuts deeper. That's the beauty of a great twist—it rewires the story retroactively.

Don't worry if your twist feels messy at first. Use ChatGPT to clean it up and strengthen the logic. Ask, "How can I plant clues in earlier scenes that foreshadow this twist without giving it away?" and you'll get subtle setups you can add during your rewrite pass. At the end of the day, the midpoint twist is your chance to turn the volume up on the entire story. It's the *oh no* moment. The game-changer. The scene that takes the story from interesting to unforgettable. It's the point where your action-adventure stops being just a ride and starts becoming a reckoning.

Because the best twists don't just spin the plot. They knock the wind out of your hero, force them to stand up again, and charge into the storm knowing that this time, it's not just dangerous...

It's *personal.*

Chase Scenes, Fight Scenes, and Near Misses

If there's one thing that defines a good action-adventure story, it's momentum. The feeling that something is always about to happen—or already *is* happening—and the hero is barely holding on. That's where chase scenes, fight scenes, and near misses come in. These aren't just the spice in the story—they're the fuel. They inject adrenaline, test your characters in real time, and create the kind of pulse-pounding tension that keeps the reader or viewer locked in. When done well, they do more than just thrill—they move the story, reveal character, and raise stakes. When done poorly, they feel like filler. So let's talk about how to get these scenes right.

Let's start with the **chase scene**. A great chase scene is built on geography, urgency, and unpredictability. It could be on foot, in a car, through a jungle, across rooftops, underwater, in the sky, or even through time—but no matter where or how it happens, it needs to do one thing: escalate. The pursuer gets closer. The environment becomes more dangerous. The options shrink. The escape route twists. The chase isn't just about running—it's about *decision-making under pressure*. A chase tells us what the hero prioritizes, fears, and risks. Do they run toward a trap to save someone? Do they create a distraction to help someone else get away? That's character in motion.

The setting is your best friend in a chase. You want obstacles. Tight spaces. Hazards. People in the way. Doors that don't open. Markets full of produce to knock over. Use the terrain like a puzzle. Ask ChatGPT for help like, "Give me a chase sequence through a crowded bazaar," and you'll get a mix of action beats, environment interaction, and tension-builders you can plug directly into your scene.

Next up: **the fight scene**. Fights are about more than who wins—they're about *how* each character fights. Are they brutal? Precise? Reckless? Reluctant? Does the fight reveal fear, anger, shame, control, or desperation? The best fight scenes aren't just choreography—they're *character studies*. Think of the difference between two enemies trying to kill each other, and two friends forced to fight under duress. Same punches, totally different emotional weight.

Keep fights physical and visceral. Don't over-explain the moves. Show what matters—the sound of a rib cracking, the sting of sweat in the eyes, the dizziness after a hard hit. Momentum is key. The best fights shift. One person gains ground, then loses it. Something in the environment changes. A weapon is lost. A distraction gives the upper hand. A line of dialogue cuts deeper than any blow. Ask ChatGPT, "Give me a fight scene in a collapsing warehouse," and you'll get a structured battle that you can customize for your character and style.

And now, the underrated but extremely effective **near miss**. These are the scenes that *almost* go wrong. The tension is high, the danger is real, and just when the character seems doomed—something saves them. Maybe it's cleverness. Maybe it's luck. Maybe it's someone else stepping in. But the close call leaves everyone rattled, changed, and on edge.

Near misses work best when they feel like true turning points. Not just plot devices to tease danger, but moments that cost something. Maybe the hero's mistake gets someone hurt. Maybe the villain learns something new. Maybe the stakes go up not because someone died—but because they *almost did*. The power of a near miss is in the *aftermath*. That pause. That realization. That shaky breath that says, "That was too close." Use ChatGPT to brainstorm versions of this. Ask, "What's a near-death escape scenario during a mountain blizzard?" or "How can a near miss emotionally impact a character who already feels guilty?" and you'll find ways to deepen the scene beyond the action.

Let's talk rhythm. In a longer story, you don't want constant chase-fight-near miss-chase-fight. You want rhythm. Build, release, build. A chase leads to a quiet hiding spot. A fight ends in a moment of vulnerability. A near miss leads to a confrontation between characters. Action without breathing room is just noise. Space your scenes so that when they *do* hit, they hit *hard*.

Here's something that helps when writing fast: storyboard the beats before you write the full scene. Ask ChatGPT, "Outline a five-beat chase through a crumbling mine," and then write it with sensory detail and character thought layered in. Or ask, "Describe the emotional arc of a rooftop duel between former allies," and now your fight isn't just physical—it's dramatic.

And remember: these scenes are opportunities to reinforce theme. If your story is about trust, let the chase involve a betrayal. If it's about redemption, let the fight be a refusal to kill. If it's about identity, let the near miss force the hero to choose between the mask they wear and the person they are. You don't need to spell it out—but let your action reflect your deeper message.

Visually, all three of these scenes benefit from contrast. Wide shots of the chase environment. Close-ups of hands slipping, eyes narrowing, fists tightening. Silence before the punch. Echoes in the chase. The sudden slam of reality when the near miss lands. Let the rhythm of the writing match the chaos or the pause. Short sentences. Fragments. Then, when the dust settles, take your time. Let the audience feel what the characters feel.

In one-day writing mode, these scenes can be your lifeline. They keep you moving. They give you anchors. They keep your story from sagging. And with ChatGPT at your fingertips, you're never stuck. Just ask for new obstacles, reversals, emotional wrinkles, or environments, and you'll always have something fresh to throw your characters into.

So chase them through fire. Make them fight in the rain. Let them almost fall, almost die, almost give up—but not quite. And in that razor-thin space between danger and disaster, you'll find the heart of the action-adventure story beating louder than ever.

Using ChatGPT to Brainstorm Twists You Never Saw Coming

In the world of action-adventure storytelling, twists are gold. They're the moments that flip the story on its head, drop jaws, make hearts race, and force your characters—and your audience—to see everything differently. But here's the thing: when you're writing fast, like crafting an entire action-adventure story in a single day, coming up with clever, original twists on your own can feel like trying to build a roller coaster while riding it. That's where ChatGPT becomes your secret weapon. Not just a writing assistant—but your personal twist factory.

Twists don't need to be gimmicks. In fact, the best ones aren't. They feel natural, inevitable *in hindsight*, and emotionally charged. They work because they're born out of the logic of the world you've created—just hidden behind smoke and mirrors until the perfect moment. The key is asking the right questions early, and letting ChatGPT help you brainstorm multiple paths for each story beat before you lock anything down. You're not just trying to write a surprise. You're trying to make the story *deeper* through shock.

Let's start at the root. Ask ChatGPT, "What's a twist that would completely reframe my action-adventure story if the main character is a treasure hunter searching for an ancient artifact?" You'll probably get a dozen different angles. The artifact is fake. It's cursed. It's already been found. It's being used as bait. Or the treasure hunter is actually the villain and doesn't know it. One of those might land like lightning. One might spark a better idea. Either way, you've just leapfrogged hours of mental strain in a single question.

The best twists often fall into a few categories—reversals of motive, identity, information, loyalty, and goal. You can break these categories down one by one and have ChatGPT help you generate options for each. For example:

- "Give me five possible character identity twists for a former military hero."
- "What are some villain motivation twists that aren't based on revenge or power?"
- "What's a twist that turns an ally into an unexpected antagonist?"

Sometimes you'll get familiar ideas—but tweak the context and they'll feel fresh. Other times you'll get something wild and unexpected, and that's where the real juice is. ChatGPT doesn't get fatigued or biased. It can throw twenty curveballs in a minute and never ask for coffee.

Here's the fun part: you can also reverse-engineer a twist. Instead of starting with plot, start with the impact. Ask, "Give me a twist that will break the hero's heart and change their mission entirely," or "Give me a twist that makes the audience realize they've been rooting for the wrong side." Now your twist is driven by emotion or theme—not just plot mechanics. These are the ones that really stick.

Want to get even more specific? You can feed ChatGPT a setup. Let's say your story so far has the hero and a charming local guide searching a sunken shipwreck in the Caribbean. Ask, "What's a plot twist that could happen in this setting involving betrayal, lost history, and a hidden agenda?" You'll get scenario-based suggestions that fit organically into the story you're already building.

And if you're stuck in the middle of the story and it's feeling too predictable, ChatGPT can inject chaos on command. Just say, "Give me three plot twists that could happen right now to shake up this story," and it will offer directions you might never have imagined. Maybe the villain's not after the artifact—they're after the *person* who's holding it. Maybe the sunken ship isn't a wreck—it's a decoy. Maybe the map was planted years ago by someone trying to lure the hero into a trap for personal revenge. Boom—your second act just got teeth.

You can also use ChatGPT to brainstorm smaller, more subtle twists. These are the ones that don't rewire the whole story but add layers to scenes or characters. Ask, "What's a small twist that could happen during a simple weapons deal in a back alley?" or "Give me a character twist that makes the comic relief unexpectedly essential to the plot." These kinds of moments create tension and surprise without needing to overhaul the narrative. They're the seasoning between the big story bombs.

A great technique is to chain multiple twists together. Ask ChatGPT to do this directly. "Create a three-twist sequence where each twist builds on the last, starting with a simple betrayal and ending in a major reveal about the hero's past." This kind of layered approach is what keeps an action-adventure story flying high all the way to the end. First you give the audience what they expect. Then you flip it. Then you flip the flip.

Even your climax can benefit from one final twist—and ChatGPT can help shape that too. Ask, "What's a climactic twist that ties back to something from the opening scene and changes how the entire story is understood?" These are the kind of surprises that make your ending feel earned and unforgettable. They loop your story into something tight and complete.

Don't worry about using all the ideas ChatGPT gives you. The goal isn't to include every twist—it's to find *the right ones.* The ones that feel like the story couldn't exist without them. The ones that push your characters into new territory. The ones that make your reader sit back and say, "No way. That *actually* just happened."

If you're writing a full story in one day, this process can save you hours of hair-pulling and page-tearing. You can spend fifteen minutes tossing ideas back and forth with ChatGPT and walk away with a plot twist that changes your entire second act—or even your theme.

So use this tool the way your hero uses a grappling hook, a lockpick, or a smoke bomb: to break through barriers, escape cliché, and sneak into the story's deeper layers. Trust your instincts—but let ChatGPT be the spark when your mind stalls. And when your twist hits, it won't just surprise your readers.

It'll surprise *you*. And that's when you know it's good.

Dialogue Passes: Punching Up the Banter

In an action-adventure story, the bullets might fly, the buildings might crumble, and the hero might barely survive—but what really sticks in the reader's memory? The banter. The one-liners. The zingers delivered mid-chase. That sharp, unexpected joke in a moment of tension. Dialogue, especially witty, fast-paced, character-defining dialogue, is what makes your story come alive between the explosions. It gives your characters charm, chemistry, and authenticity. And the good news? You can always punch it up—even if you're writing the entire story in one mad dash of a day.

A "dialogue pass" is exactly what it sounds like. Once you've written your scenes, you go back and do a second sweep with one purpose: to make the dialogue sharper, funnier, more human, and more memorable. This is where you infuse rhythm, voice, humor, and energy into your characters' lines. And when you're moving fast, ChatGPT is the perfect banter co-writer sitting right beside you, tossing out lines until one hits just right.

Let's break this down, starting with *why* you should do a dialogue pass. Even in the most tightly plotted action scene, dialogue is what gives your story personality. Without it, your characters blur together. With it, they pop. It's the banter between the cynical hero and the idealistic partner that makes their relationship shine. It's the villain's smug remark before triggering the trap that makes them unforgettable. It's the throwaway line the hero mutters after narrowly escaping death that makes readers smile in the middle of a high-stakes moment.

So what's the secret to punching up banter? It starts with *voice*. Each character should sound distinct. If you can swap their dialogue and it still works, you've got a problem. Give your characters quirks—maybe one talks in metaphors, one is dry and clipped, another rambles when nervous. If you're stuck, ask ChatGPT, "Write three different speech styles for a sarcastic ex-mercenary, a rookie cop, and a smooth-talking tech thief," and you'll start to see how personality shapes phrasing.

Then comes *timing*. Banter is rhythm. Think of it like music. Short bursts. Set up and payoff. Interruption. Overlap. Silence. The best banter isn't two people delivering monologues—it's tennis. Back and forth, fast, clever, and unexpected. Ask ChatGPT, "Write a banter exchange between two rivals forced to work together while defusing a bomb," and you'll get examples of dialogue that bounce, spark, and surprise.

Context also matters. Banter during downtime is different from banter during danger. A bored conversation on a long boat ride can be filled with jabs and backstory. A frantic exchange in a gunfight might be clipped and ironic. But both should feel real, and both should reflect the stress, tension, or absurdity of the moment. Try asking ChatGPT, "Give me sarcastic but panicked dialogue between two characters trapped in an elevator during a shootout," and you'll get lines that walk the tightrope between fear and comedy.

Another great use of dialogue passes is to *layer emotion underneath the banter*. Sometimes, the funniest or sharpest lines are really cover for something deeper—regret, fear, guilt. A character might joke about being left behind, but underneath, they're still hurt. Let ChatGPT help you find that subtext. Say, "Write a dialogue exchange where one character pretends they don't care they were betrayed, but clearly does," and now your banter has teeth.

Want to give a scene more energy? Toss in some tension-laced sarcasm. Want to deepen the bond between two characters without a full conversation? A single exchanged look and a deadpan line can do it. Want to make your villain unsettling? Let them be calm, polite, even charming—while doing something monstrous. ChatGPT can help find those twists. "Write villain dialogue that sounds friendly but implies a serious threat," and suddenly your bad guy's words carry chill.

Let's talk *callbacks*. These are great in action-adventure. If a character says something early in the story that seems like a throwaway line, you can bring it back later in a completely different context. It becomes a shared in-joke, a moment of triumph, or a gut-punch. Ask ChatGPT, "Give me a line of dialogue that could be reused later with a completely different meaning," and you've got a thread you can tug through the story.

And sometimes, the best way to punch up your dialogue is just to have fun with it. Ask ChatGPT, "Write ten over-the-top one-liners for a hero jumping from a moving train," and you'll get a list you can cherry-pick or remix. Or, "Give me sarcastic responses to a villain's long-winded speech," and suddenly your protagonist doesn't just survive—they roast their enemy in the process.

Remember that a dialogue pass isn't about adding more lines—it's about making the ones you've got *sing*. That one perfect comeback, that unexpected bit of dry humor, that tension-breaking wisecrack—that's what keeps your reader connected to the character, even as bullets fly.

And it's not just about being funny. It's about voice. Vulnerability. Connection. Banter builds trust. Banter builds rhythm. Banter makes danger fun and stakes feel personal.

So after you've written your action, your twists, your chase scenes, and explosions—circle back. Highlight your dialogue. See what's flat. See what's trying too hard. See what's almost there. Then call in ChatGPT and say, "Let's punch this up."

Because sometimes the most explosive thing in an action-adventure story isn't a grenade or a rooftop fall...

It's a line that hits so hard, you have to read it twice.

High-Tech or Low-Fi? Designing Your Story's Gear

In an action-adventure story, the gear your characters use is more than just tools—it's personality. Whether your hero is scaling cliffs with magnetic gloves, hacking into encrypted systems with a homemade laptop, or fighting with a broken-down machete taped together with duct tape, their equipment says something about who they are, how they operate, and what kind of world they move through. And one of the first decisions you'll make when building your action-adventure world is this: do you want high-tech... or low-fi?

It's not just an aesthetic choice. It changes how your characters solve problems, how your action scenes play out, and what kind of tension you're working with. And it influences the *tone* of your story in a big way. A sleek, gadget-heavy spy thriller feels completely different than a gritty survival trek through the jungle with nothing but a knife and a hand-drawn map. Both work. But mixing the two without intention? That's where things get messy.

When you're writing your story in one day, you don't have time to second-guess every choice. So the key is to pick your gear philosophy early—then let it ripple out naturally into every action beat. If you're not sure what fits your story, this is where ChatGPT becomes a total cheat code. Just ask, "What kind of gear would suit a fast-paced action story set in a flooded post-apocalyptic city?" and it'll give you equipment ideas that reflect the setting, mood, and plot.

So let's break down the difference.

High-tech gear usually implies advanced environments, organized teams, well-funded operations, or sci-fi influences. Think laser-cutting devices, cloaking suits, AI-powered drones, retinal scanners, or satellites tracking every move. This kind of story feels sleek, calculated, and sophisticated. The tension often comes from precision and stakes. The gear allows you to build clever set-pieces—breaking into impossible places, stopping weapons before they launch, pulling off complex heists.

But the downside? High-tech can sometimes feel too clean. Too safe. If your hero has a gadget for every problem, the danger starts to feel low-stakes. So if you're going high-tech, make the tech unreliable. It breaks. It gets hacked. It runs out of power. That's when things get interesting. Ask ChatGPT, "Give me three ways a high-tech gadget could fail at the worst possible moment," and suddenly your hero isn't just using gear—they're scrambling to survive *despite* it.

Low-fi gear, on the other hand, is all about improvisation, scarcity, and grit. This is your Indiana Jones, Mad Max, Tomb Raider zone—where the hero might be held together with rope, instinct, and luck. Low-fi gear means machetes, lockpicks, flare guns, horses, cracked binoculars, and homemade explosives. It's more physical, more grounded, and often more intense. The gear *feels* like it's part of the world—worn, dirty, maybe even rusted.

The advantage here is it pushes your characters to be resourceful. They don't have a tracking device—they follow footprints. They don't have a jetpack—they steal a dirt bike and ride through a thunderstorm. These stories often feel more human, more desperate, and more raw. You can ask ChatGPT, "List ten pieces of low-fi gear a hero might carry into a jungle temple," and build an entire sequence around using each one in unexpected ways.

The sweet spot? Sometimes it's both. One of the most interesting dynamics in gear design is the *contrast*. The high-tech villain vs. the low-fi hero. The digital plan that gets ruined, forcing the characters to go analog. The agent with the bleeding-edge briefcase full of gadgets who's forced to fight with a chair leg when it all goes sideways. These moments are gold. Ask ChatGPT, "How can a low-fi hero outsmart a high-tech antagonist in a desert setting?" and you'll get ideas that lean into brains over budget.

The gear should always be tied to character. A cocky hacker might carry a souped-up phone rigged to breach firewalls in seconds. A stoic ex-soldier might carry a custom knife with notches for every life saved. A globe-trotting thief might have a collapsible grappling hook disguised as jewelry. And the gear can evolve, too. Maybe your character starts with nothing, then builds their kit over time. Or maybe they begin reliant on high-tech tools, but have to learn to survive without them. That's a character arc *through gear.*

Even if your gear is fictional, ground it in logic. If your villain has a drone swarm, how do they control it? What powers it? If your hero has a wrist-mounted grappling line, how far can it reach? Does it run on gas or a hidden coil system? These tiny choices make the world feel real. Ask ChatGPT, "Explain how a magnetic climbing glove could realistically work in a sci-fi action story," and you can weave that detail into a tense rooftop escape.

And remember, gear can be emotional too. The hero's father's old compass. A bullet-scarred canteen from a past mission. A lucky coin. These aren't just props—they're memory, history, and vulnerability. When those items get lost, broken, or repurposed, it hurts. That's story. Ask ChatGPT, "Give me five sentimental gear items that a reluctant hero might carry," and now your gear has *soul.*

When you get stuck writing an action scene, let the gear drive it. "How can my character use a single flare to escape a mountain ambush?" or "What's a clever use of duct tape in a high-speed chase?" The answers you get from ChatGPT won't just solve your scene—they'll reveal who your character is under pressure.

So, choose your lane. Sleek and futuristic? Gritty and improvised? A mix of both? Whatever it is, let the gear become part of your story's heartbeat. Let it solve problems. Create new ones. Shape the tension. Reveal the hero.

Because in action-adventure, when the bullets stop flying and the dust settles, the audience might forget which line came first or how many explosions there were...

But they'll remember the character who built a zipline from a seatbelt and a broken broomstick. Or the agent who disarmed a bomb with chewing gum and sarcasm.

The gear they carry? That's the story they leave behind.

Dangerous Situations and How to Keep Them Believable

One of the best things about writing action-adventure is throwing your characters into truly dangerous, pulse-pounding situations—death-defying stunts, high-stakes escapes, near-impossible missions, traps, betrayals, natural disasters, enemy fire, collapsing buildings, and the occasional swordfight on a moving vehicle. The danger is what gives the genre its heartbeat. But here's the trick: danger only works when it *feels* real. When it's grounded in something the audience believes, or at least *wants* to believe. Because the moment your story starts breaking its own rules or making your reader roll their eyes, the tension snaps—and it's hard to get back.

So how do you keep your dangerous situations thrilling *and* believable—especially when writing your story at high speed in one day? You anchor everything in logic, consequence, and character. And with ChatGPT by your side, you can build, pressure-test, and troubleshoot any moment of chaos to make sure it hits hard and lands clean.

Let's start with this idea: **the danger has to matter.** If your hero crashes a motorcycle, falls off a balcony, gets caught in a fire, and walks away without a limp, your audience starts checking out. The tension is fake. They know your character's invincible. The key isn't to avoid danger—it's to let the danger cost something. A wound. A scar. A loss. A broken trust. A moment of hesitation that haunts them. Ask ChatGPT, "What are believable consequences of surviving a helicopter crash in the Arctic?" and suddenly your action scene has gravity.

Plausibility doesn't mean realism—it means internal consistency. James Bond survives things no real human could, but within *his* world, those stunts follow a certain logic. If you've established that your hero is tough, trained, or just very lucky, the audience will accept a lot—but you have to make the action feel *earned.* If they dive from a burning rooftop into a river and swim to safety, show the exhaustion. Show the cold, the coughing, the moment they barely make it. Don't just teleport them to dry land. That's where believability lives—in the *struggle*, not just the escape.

Setups make payoffs feel earned. If your character suddenly escapes an explosion using a fireproof blanket they never had before, the audience calls foul. But if you showed them grabbing it earlier, or established they always carry one in their kit, then it works. Plant what they need. Even if it's subtle. A quick line. A background detail. Then when the danger hits, they survive not by luck, but by preparation. ChatGPT can help you with this: "How can I subtly set up a tool the hero will use to escape a burning warehouse later?" and you'll get breadcrumbs to leave in early scenes.

Use environment to your advantage. One of the easiest ways to create believable danger is to use the setting. A desert with no shade or water. A mountain with a shifting ice shelf. A jungle teeming with insects and disease. These natural hazards don't need to be explained—they just *are*. And they're universal. We all understand dehydration, exposure, gravity, sharp objects, and panicked decisions under pressure. Ask ChatGPT, "What environmental dangers can escalate a scene set in a derelict oil rig during a storm?" and you've got a buffet of believable chaos ready to go.

Mistakes create tension. Nobody gets it right every time. Let your characters mess up—take the wrong turn, misjudge the jump, forget to reload. These flaws make them real, and the danger more believable. Think about the last great action movie you saw. Did the hero always win clean? Or did they fumble, get lucky, or pull something off by the skin of their teeth? ChatGPT can help here: "What are believable mistakes a hero could make while sneaking through enemy territory?" and you'll get options that heighten tension without breaking your story.

Let danger reflect character. If your hero is cocky, let their overconfidence lead them into a trap. If they're hesitant, let that moment of indecision cause a loss. The danger becomes more than just physical—it becomes emotional. That's when it starts to matter. Ask ChatGPT, "How can a character's internal flaw lead them into a dangerous situation?" and you'll get a layered approach that makes the danger more personal.

Don't overplay the invincibility card. Yes, action heroes survive a lot. But let them get hurt. Let them lose. Let them panic. That doesn't make them weak—it makes them *human.* When your hero limps through the final battle, scarred and shaken, we *feel* the cost. And if they survive because of grit, brains, or help from an unlikely ally—not just dumb luck—it's way more satisfying. Ask ChatGPT, "What's a believable way for an outnumbered hero to survive a shootout in an abandoned village?" and you'll get tactics that feel grounded, not godlike.

Stack the odds. Then twist them. Danger is most believable when it builds. First it's a storm. Then it's enemy scouts. Then the fuel runs out. Then the map gets destroyed. Layer problems on top of each other until the hero isn't just trying to win—they're trying to survive with *anything* left. That kind of pressure makes even simple choices feel massive. You can tell ChatGPT, "Build a three-layer danger scenario for an escape from an underground lab," and you'll get a blueprint for a scene that escalates with each step.

Use the aftermath to sell the danger. Don't end a scene and pretend it never happened. Let the burns sting. Let the broken wrist make climbing impossible. Let the hero flinch at the sound of gunfire after a close call. These details don't slow the story—they *deepen* it. The danger echoes. That's what keeps it believable. Ask ChatGPT, "What are lingering effects of a near-death underwater escape?" and you'll be able to write scenes that live *after* the action.

At the end of the day, writing danger that feels real is all about grounding it in physicality, emotion, and consequence. You don't need to hold back on scale—go big, go wild—but build the scaffolding under your spectacle. Let your audience feel the threat, not just watch it. Let your characters *pay* for surviving.

Because when the danger feels earned, the survival feels powerful.

And that's when your action-adventure story stops being just a thrill ride—and becomes a story of *endurance, transformation,* and *truth under fire.*

The Hero's Journey with an Action-Adventure Spin

We've all heard of the Hero's Journey—the timeless structure found in myths, epics, and just about every blockbuster franchise ever made. But when you take that classic arc and strap a rocket to it, you get something else entirely: the Hero's Journey with an action-adventure spin. It's still about growth, challenge, transformation—but now it comes with chase scenes, deadly traps, ticking clocks, near-death experiences, explosive reveals, and a whole lot of sweat and grit. And when you're writing a story in one day, using this structure gives you an automatic roadmap. No guesswork, just forward motion.

Let's walk through the beats of the Hero's Journey and see how they shift when filtered through the lens of action-adventure storytelling.

It begins with the **Ordinary World**, but in action-adventure, this world is often a little heightened. Your hero might be an ex-soldier running a fishing boat, a brilliant but broke archeologist, a jaded spy doing freelance work, or even a rookie with no clue what they're about to be pulled into. The trick is to show their comfort zone—then make it clear they don't belong there anymore. Action heroes are often misfits, restless souls, or people with ghosts they're trying to outrun. Ask ChatGPT, "What are some compelling ordinary world setups for a reluctant adventurer?" and you'll have solid launchpads to work from.

Then comes the **Call to Adventure**, which in this genre usually shows up like a punch to the face. It might be a mysterious message, a botched job, a stolen artifact, a kidnapping, or an offer that can't be refused. The danger is real, and the stakes are instantly high. There's not much time for thinking—only reacting. In action-adventure, the call often kicks in with physical momentum: someone's already chasing, something's already exploding. You can say to ChatGPT, "Write an action-packed call to adventure involving a sabotage during a gala," and you'll get a scene that shoves your hero out the door.

The **Refusal of the Call** can be internal or external. Maybe the hero turns down the mission. Maybe someone tries to stop them. Maybe they think they're not ready. In action-adventure, this beat is often brief—it's a hesitation while loading weapons, a look in the mirror, a call they don't return. It adds a human pause before the wild ride. Let ChatGPT help you sharpen it: "Give me a short emotional beat where a hero almost backs out of a dangerous mission."

Next is the **Meeting with the Mentor**, but in this genre, mentors can come in all flavors—grizzled veterans, retired spies, mysterious old enemies, or even someone the hero is forced to protect but ends up learning from. In action-adventure, mentors often get killed, betrayed, or left behind, pushing the hero to stand on their own. They're rarely just wise sages. They're people with scars and unfinished business. You can ask ChatGPT, "Create a flawed but memorable mentor for a treasure hunter," and you'll get dynamic personalities to shape your story around.

Crossing the **Threshold** is often literal in action-adventure. The plane takes off. The boat leaves the harbor. The forbidden zone is entered. From here on out, the world changes. The enemies are real. The rules shift. The danger is personal. This is where the story stops building and starts *burning*. Ask ChatGPT, "Describe an intense threshold-crossing moment for a reluctant hero," and let that be the ignition point for Act Two.

Then comes **Tests, Allies, and Enemies**—the fun, messy middle. This is where your action sequences come in. The fights, the chases, the puzzles, the quicksand, the lies. New characters show up. Some will help, some will hurt, some will do both. In action-adventure, these scenes often overlap—your hero might have to figure out who to trust while dodging bullets. Keep the tension high and the alliances shifting. Ask ChatGPT, "Give me three escalating challenges a hero faces in a jungle temple," and you've got momentum built in.

Approach to the Inmost Cave is when things turn serious. The goal is close. The team is smaller. The tension is thick. The hero has changed, whether they admit it or not. In action-adventure, this is often the calm before the storm—a moment to regroup, reflect, and prepare for whatever's inside. Maybe it's a tomb. A fortress. A server room beneath a volcano. Whatever it is, the audience should feel that the real danger hasn't even started yet. Ask ChatGPT, "Describe a tense approach scene to a hostile location," and you can set the mood in seconds.

The Ordeal is the centrepiece of the journey—the moment that tests everything. The fight against the villain. The moment of betrayal. The impossible escape. The brush with death. In action-adventure, this is your big set-piece. It's physical. It's messy. But it's also emotional. It's not just about winning—it's about *who* the hero is becoming. Ask ChatGPT, "Write an ordeal scene where the hero chooses someone else's life over the mission," and you'll tie character and action together.

The Reward comes next. Maybe they get the thing they were chasing. Maybe they don't—but they gain knowledge, clarity, or strength. In some action stories, this is a literal object. In others, it's a truth. A name. A key. A confession. It's what they need to go into the final act with a purpose.

But first, they face **The Road Back**—and in action-adventure, this is never simple. The villain makes a final play. The hero's escape is blocked. Everything they gained might be lost. This is your ticking clock moment, your final race, your gut-punch twist. It's the setup for your **Climax**.

The Resurrection is the final battle—the moment the hero dies metaphorically and comes back changed. In action-adventure, it's the explosion-filled showdown where all the threads collide. But underneath the chaos, it's about resolution. The inner journey ends here. The coward becomes brave. The loner saves someone. The vengeful one lets go. Ask ChatGPT, "Design a climax where the hero sacrifices their goal to save their values," and you'll find the perfect close.

And finally, **Return with the Elixir**. The hero goes home—or maybe finds a new one. The world might not be saved, but something inside the hero is. In action-adventure, this beat doesn't have to be a quiet fade-out. Maybe the hero drops the artifact in the ocean. Maybe they fake their death. Maybe they walk off into the jungle, smiling for the first time. Ask ChatGPT, "Write an emotionally satisfying final scene for a hero who can't go back to their old life," and land your story with weight and wonder.

When you use the Hero's Journey as your skeleton, and wrap it in action, stakes, danger, and heart—you're building something timeless that also punches like a blockbuster. So don't just run from explosion to explosion. Let the journey shape the hero. Let the danger sharpen the soul. Let the story *mean something*.

And if you're doing it in one day, don't stress—just follow the steps, ride the momentum, and let ChatGPT keep you on the trail.

Because in the end, the adventure isn't just about what the hero finds...

It's about who they become.

Writing the "One Day" Action Story

Let's be honest—writing an entire action-adventure story in one day sounds like madness. And yet, it's not only possible, it can be wildly effective, creatively freeing, and surprisingly fun. Especially when you're using ChatGPT as your co-pilot. The key is knowing how to approach it, how to use momentum instead of overthinking, and how to harness speed as a storytelling weapon. Because the "one day" action story isn't about perfection—it's about energy. About instinct. About riding the wave of adrenaline just like your characters are.

The secret sauce here is structure plus spontaneity. You want to have a rough map of where you're going, but you don't want to build every bridge before you get there. You want to know the kind of story you're telling, the hero at the center, and the tone—gritty and grounded, or slick and globe-trotting. After that? Let the story run wild.

Start by giving yourself a tight premise. You don't have time to wander through subplots and side quests. This is a mission, not a memoir. One goal. One enemy. One central conflict. Maybe it's "stop the bomb before midnight," or "retrieve the stolen prototype before it leaves the country," or "survive the jungle long enough to make the extraction point." The tighter the objective, the more room you have to stretch the action. Ask ChatGPT, "Give me five fast, high-stakes action story premises that take place in one day," and you'll be off and running before your coffee gets cold.

Because yes—your *story* takes place in one day, too. That's part of the appeal. A single explosive day in the life of someone who never asked for this but is now knee-deep in danger, betrayal, and ticking clocks. The time crunch creates built-in tension. Everything has to happen fast. Decisions have to be made on instinct. There's no time to rest. Just like you, as the writer. You're telling the story as if it's unfolding in real-time.

Next, think about your opening. You don't need ten pages of setup. You need an explosion. A betrayal. A dead drop. An ambush. Your protagonist should be in motion by paragraph two. No need for a detailed backstory. The character reveals themselves through the way they act under pressure. You can always sprinkle backstory in as you go—just ask ChatGPT, "What's a compelling way to show a hero's past trauma during a high-stakes escape?" and let the story layer itself.

One of the best tricks in one-day writing is using **movement** as your narrative glue. Your characters are always on the move—across rooftops, through tunnels, out of sinking vehicles. Each location introduces a new obstacle. A new threat. A new ally or enemy. This keeps you from getting bogged down in exposition and forces you to keep the story lean and sharp. Every scene has a purpose. If it doesn't raise the stakes, complicate the plan, or test the hero—it's gone.

Now let's talk pacing. In an action-adventure story set over a single day, pacing isn't just important—it's everything. You want breathless, but not exhausting. That means you need rhythm. Follow each high-octane sequence with a breather. A quiet moment. A hidden room. A whispered conversation. A moral choice. Then back into the chaos. Ask ChatGPT, "What are effective low-tension beats that still build character during a fast-paced action story?" and you'll find places to let the story breathe without slowing it down.

Your antagonist should also be active. You don't have time for a villain waiting in a lair. They should be on the move, pressing the hero, staying a step ahead or showing up where they're least expected. That back-and-forth chase between protagonist and antagonist creates natural propulsion. Ask ChatGPT, "Give me a dynamic villain who can challenge the hero mentally and physically," and you'll add dimension to the cat-and-mouse dynamic.

Because you're writing the whole thing in one day, keep your cast tight. A main character, a partner or foil, a clear villain, and maybe one or two wild cards. More than that, and your dialogue slows down. You want each character to reflect an aspect of the theme or the hero's internal struggle. You can build these fast. Just ask ChatGPT, "Create a trio of characters for a one-day rescue mission in hostile territory," and you'll get a ready-to-roll team with quirks and tension.

Endings matter more when you've written fast. Don't fizzle out. Land hard. You want the climax to be the emotional and physical payoff of everything that's come before. The final fight, the final choice, the final transformation. Has the hero grown? Changed? Lost something? Gained clarity? These moments matter more than the explosions. Ask ChatGPT, "Write a high-stakes ending where the hero sacrifices their mission for something more important," and wrap your story with meaning.

And when you finish that last line—resist the urge to tinker. You can clean it later. Right now, you've done something incredible. You wrote a full-blown, heart-pounding, character-driven action story in a single day. You followed the chaos. You made choices on instinct. You kept the pedal down. That's the point. Not perfection—*momentum*.

The beauty of the one-day action story is that it teaches you speed, focus, and clarity. It cuts the fat. It forces you to make decisions and trust them. And with ChatGPT as your partner, you never run dry. You're never stuck. You're never out of fuel. Just ask, adapt, and keep moving.

So the next time someone says you can't write a gripping action-adventure story in 24 hours, just smile.

Because you already did.

Creating Conflicts that Can't Be Ignored

At the heart of every unforgettable action-adventure story lies conflict that demands attention. Not just loud conflict. Not just conflict that triggers explosions and fistfights. But *compelling, inescapable* conflict—something that grabs your protagonist by the collar and refuses to let go. These are the kinds of conflicts that push your characters forward even when they want to turn back, that raise stakes every time the hero catches their breath, and that pull readers or viewers so deep into the story they forget they're watching or reading. In a one-day writing sprint, these conflicts are your power source. Without them, your plot might move, but it won't *matter*.

So how do you build conflict that won't be ignored?

You start by raising the personal stakes. Conflict becomes unshakable when it taps into something that *matters deeply* to your protagonist It's not just about stopping the bomb—it's about stopping the bomb *because their sister is inside the building*. Not just catching the villain—but catching the villain *because they know what the hero did years ago*. The mission must intersect with the character's fears, guilt, pride, or moral code. That's how you make the danger *stick*. You can ask ChatGPT, "What's a personal reason my hero would risk their life to stop a political assassination?" and you'll find the emotional tether that keeps the hero locked into the mission.

Another trick? Create *conflict with no good choices*. If your hero can take the easy way out, it's not really conflict—it's just a delayed decision. The best conflicts offer no clean solutions. Save one person or save many. Finish the job or protect a friend. Lie and live or tell the truth and die. These are the moments that force characters to reveal who they really are. In action-adventure, you can drop these choices right in the middle of chaos: a decision on a crashing plane, a split-second judgment in the middle of a shootout. Ask ChatGPT, "What are three moral dilemmas a mercenary might face during a hostage rescue mission?" and watch the tension double.

Layered conflict is even better. The external threat (the armed convoy, the erupting volcano, the ticking bomb) is real, but so is the internal tension (a betrayal, a broken promise, a deep-rooted fear). You want both happening at once. Let your characters argue while climbing a mountain. Let a grudge boil over during a fire-fight. Let old wounds reopen while handcuffed together in enemy territory. Ask ChatGPT, "What's a personal conflict that could erupt between two teammates during a mission in enemy territory?" and now your scene is carrying emotional heat as well as physical risk.

Also, let your conflicts *evolve*. The best ones don't stay static. A mission that starts as a job turns into a revenge quest. A partnership turns into a rivalry. An easy win turns into an unwinnable scenario. Your hero might think they're chasing a paycheck—but halfway through, they realize they're trying to atone for something. That shift, that reveal, makes the conflict feel alive. Ask ChatGPT, "How can a bounty hunter's motivation shift from profit to redemption during a chase?" and you'll build a through-line that keeps your reader hooked.

Don't forget the antagonist. Great conflict needs a worthy opponent. Not just someone who wants to destroy things—but someone who wants *something opposite to what your hero wants.* And even better? Someone who believes *they're right.* The most magnetic villains aren't evil for the sake of it. They're clear. Convincing. Maybe even sympathetic. When their goals clash with the hero's—and when they're two sides of the same coin—the conflict becomes deeply satisfying. Ask ChatGPT, "Create an antagonist whose ideals directly oppose my hero's belief in justice," and you'll get more than just a bad guy. You'll get friction that can't be ignored.

Setting can fuel conflict, too. A crumbling city. A war zone. A sinking ship. A jungle full of booby-traps. These aren't just cool backdrops—they're built-in sources of tension. Let the environment fight your characters. Let it complicate their goals. Let it *force* them to confront their issues. Ask ChatGPT, "What environmental hazards could increase tension in a desert heist?" and you'll get fresh obstacles that keep your characters in a constant state of stress.

Time limits are also a gift in action-adventure. Nothing makes conflict tighter than a clock ticking down. Whether it's twenty-four hours to stop an assassination, one hour to rescue someone, or thirty seconds before a train hits the explosives—they force characters to act now, not later. Every decision becomes heavier. Every second wasted is a second lost. Ask ChatGPT, "How can I design a countdown scenario that builds emotional and physical pressure simultaneously?" and you'll make your conflict impossible to ignore—because time *won't* wait.

And finally, don't be afraid to let conflict hurt. Let it break relationships. Let it draw blood. Let it cost something. When danger leaves bruises and betrayal leaves silence, your story earns its tension. If your characters can walk through every explosion, argument, and mission unchanged, then the conflict didn't do its job. But if it leaves a scar—physical or emotional—it'll stick with your audience long after the scene is over.

So when you sit down to write your action-adventure story in a single day, build your engine around conflict. Make it specific. Make it personal. Make it moral. Make it burn. Ask ChatGPT when you need more heat, more tension, more edge—and keep pushing your hero into corners they don't want to be in.

Because when the conflict feels like a ticking bomb inside your characters—not just around them—you don't need to convince anyone to care.

They already do.

Antagonists with Depth, Not Just Evil Plans

In every action-adventure story, you've got danger, momentum, explosions, narrow escapes—and somewhere in the middle of all that chaos is the antagonist. The villain. The shadow. The one standing between the hero and their goal. But here's the truth: if your antagonist is just a cardboard cutout with a doomsday device and an evil laugh, your story won't hit nearly as hard as it could. For the conflict to mean something, the antagonist has to *mean* something. They need to be more than the obstacle—they need to be a presence. A worldview. A reflection of everything your hero *could* become, or already fears they are.

When you're writing a fast-paced action-adventure story in a single day, it's tempting to throw in a generic bad guy to keep the plot moving. But it doesn't take much extra time to give that antagonist some weight. And with ChatGPT in your corner, you can develop a layered villain as quickly as you can throw together an ambush or a heist.

Let's start with the biggest shift in mindset: villains don't think they're villains. They think they're *right*. They believe in something. They have a mission, a cause, a code—even if it's twisted. And they'll risk or sacrifice just as much as the hero to get what they want. The difference is what they're willing to do to achieve it.

So don't ask, "What's my villain's evil plan?" Ask, "What does my antagonist *believe* that puts them in direct opposition to the hero?" Then build from there.

You can ask ChatGPT, "What is a compelling belief system for an antagonist who wants to destroy a corrupt government?" and you'll get back motivations rooted in betrayal, disillusionment, justice gone wrong, or even revenge that almost feels justified. That's where the magic starts. Now your villain isn't evil because the story needs a villain. They're driven. They're passionate. And most importantly—they're human.

Another powerful approach? Make your antagonist a *dark mirror* of the hero. They want similar things—maybe peace, control, survival, legacy—but their methods are polar opposites. The villain does what the hero won't. Or what the hero *might*, if pushed far enough. This creates not just conflict, but philosophical tension. The hero has to win the battle without becoming what they hate. Ask ChatGPT, "How can I make my antagonist reflect the hero's internal conflict?" and you'll find ways to tie their arcs together in a way that hits deeper than bullets.

You also want to give your antagonist history. Where did they come from? What happened to them? Why do they see the world the way they do? You don't need to drop their full backstory in the middle of a chase scene, but a well-placed line or moment of vulnerability can change the audience's whole perspective. Ask ChatGPT, "What's a tragic or formative event that could explain why my villain distrusts all governments?" and now you're building complexity, not just cruelty.

Antagonists can be charming, too. In fact, they *should* be. There's something electric about a villain who's magnetic, intelligent, maybe even likeable—until you realize what they're capable of. This creates tension in scenes where the antagonist and hero are face-to-face. Dialogue becomes a chess match. Threats are veiled. Respect and loathing mix together. Ask ChatGPT, "Write a charismatic antagonist who masks violence with eloquence," and you'll get lines that drip with both civility and menace.

And don't underestimate the power of *vulnerability*. A villain who's been hurt, betrayed, or broken is far more compelling than one who's just evil for sport. Maybe they've lost someone. Maybe they've been used. Maybe they believe no one else can be trusted with power. That doesn't excuse their actions—but it *explains* them. Ask ChatGPT, "What personal loss could drive a former hero to become a global threat?" and you'll start building an antagonist whose pain feels real.

Great antagonists also evolve. They're not static. As the story moves forward, they get closer to their goal. They become more desperate. More dangerous. Or more unhinged. Maybe they start out calm and calculated, but crack when the plan falls apart. Maybe they feel victory slipping away and lash out. Maybe they grow to respect the hero—and hate them for it. Ask ChatGPT, "How can I show the psychological unraveling of a villain as their plan collapses?" and let the emotional arc play out in tandem with the action.

You can also subvert the role completely. Maybe the villain isn't who we think. Maybe the person pulling the strings is hidden until the final act. Maybe the antagonist isn't a person at all—it's a system, a curse, a belief. And the human face of it is just as trapped as the hero. Ask ChatGPT, "What are some twist reveals that could reframe the villain's role in the story?" and you'll find yourself deepening the mystery without missing a beat.

If you need to get started fast, have ChatGPT create a complete villain profile on the spot. "Build a multi-dimensional antagonist for a high-octane jungle rescue mission" will give you personality, motives, backstory, and goals—ready to drop into your plot. No wasted time, no cardboard characters.

The bottom line? In action-adventure, a great villain doesn't just want to blow something up. They want to prove a point. They want to change the world—or destroy it so something better can rise. And if they do their job right, they'll haunt the hero long after the last bullet is fired.

Because the best villains don't just stand in the way. They push the hero to the edge of who they are. And sometimes...

That's where the real adventure begins.

Getting the Hero's Motivation Right

If your action-adventure story is the engine, then the hero's motivation is the fuel. Without it, you might still have cool chase scenes, flashy fight sequences, and exotic locations—but none of it will *matter*. The hero's motivation is what makes the reader or viewer *care*. It gives weight to every decision, tension to every escape, and heart to every victory or loss. And if you're writing your story in one day, this becomes even more important. You don't have time for slow reveals or elaborate subplots. The motivation needs to be clear, compelling, and felt from the very first scene.

So let's start with the most important truth: **your hero must want something deeply**. Not casually. Not conveniently. They need to want it so badly that they're willing to go through hell to get it. Whether it's finding a missing person, clearing their name, saving a loved one, or stopping a world-ending event—it has to be personal. Even if the stakes are global, the reason to act must hit home.

You don't need a lot of space to establish this. One good line of dialogue, one flash of emotion, one visual cue—a photo in a wallet, a scar, a name whispered in pain—can do the job. You can say to ChatGPT, "Give me a short but powerful way to show a hero's motivation to find their kidnapped brother," and you'll get ideas that hit emotionally without slowing down the pacing.

Motivation and backstory are tied at the hip. Often, what the hero wants now is rooted in something they lost, failed at, or regret from the past. Maybe they weren't there when someone needed them. Maybe they walked away from a cause and now they're being pulled back. Maybe they've been living in the shadows, and now something forces them into the light. Ask ChatGPT, "What kind of past failure could drive a reluctant hero into a new mission?" and you'll discover emotional threads that add depth to every action scene.

Sometimes the motivation isn't even fully known to the hero. They start the mission for one reason—but as the story unfolds, a deeper reason reveals itself. Maybe they're not just chasing justice—they're seeking redemption. Not just saving someone—they're trying to forgive themselves. This layered approach gives you room to grow the character as the plot explodes around them. Ask ChatGPT, "What hidden motivation might surface during a high-stakes survival story?" and you'll uncover the internal journey beneath the external chaos.

Your hero's motivation should also **collide with their flaw**. This is where tension lives. If they want to save someone but are afraid of intimacy, that conflict drives decisions. If they crave justice but have a history of violence, their path is never clean. Let the motivation pull them forward and the flaw pull them back. Let the story be the battlefield between the two. Ask ChatGPT "What's a character flaw that would complicate a hero's need to expose government corruption?" and you'll find the perfect storm of intention and conflict.

What's crucial in action-adventure is that the hero's motivation *fuels action*. It's not just emotional weight—it's a reason to fight, run, climb, bleed, and refuse to quit. The hero doesn't have time to mope. They have time to act. But that action must come from somewhere honest. Even if the hero is stoic, their choices should scream their motivation. The reader or viewer should be able to feel what's at stake even when no one is saying it out loud.

One trick that helps is asking: *What happens if the hero fails?* Not just in terms of plot, but in terms of their personal stakes. If they lose the mission, what else do they lose? Their sense of self? Their last chance at redemption? Someone they love? This sharpens the urgency and keeps them in motion even when everything goes wrong. You can ask ChatGPT, "What are three layered consequences for a hero failing to stop a citywide bio-attack?" and you'll quickly have pressure on every level—physical, emotional, and moral.

Make sure the antagonist's goal challenges the hero's motivation. If your hero wants peace and the villain wants chaos, that's surface-level. But if your hero wants peace and the villain *believes* chaos is the only way to get it, now the conflict is personal. That's how motivations drive character dynamics. They're not just opposing goals—they're opposing philosophies. Ask ChatGPT, "How can a villain's goal force the hero to question their own motivation?" and now you're in territory where even the hero isn't sure if they're doing the right thing.

You don't need long speeches or tearful monologues. A great action-adventure keeps motivation active. Let the hero's choices reflect their drive. Let their sacrifices make sense. Let their breaking points feel earned. If the hero has to choose between winning and staying true to themselves, that's when motivation *matters most*.

When writing fast, use ChatGPT to test your choices. Ask, "Does this motivation support the kind of action scenes I want to write?" or "How can I strengthen a weak motivation for a reluctant hero in a prison escape plot?" The answers will help you dial in the emotional core of your story without grinding the momentum.

Because in the end, it's not the explosions, gadgets, or body count that make people remember your story—it's the *why*. Why does your hero keep going when every bone in their body says stop? Why do they dive into the burning building, the collapsing tunnel, the enemy-infested jungle?

The answer is the motivation. Get that right, and everything else—every leap, fight, loss, and win—will land harder, ring louder, and echo longer.

Emotional Arcs beneath the Gunfire

In the thick of an action-adventure story, it's easy to let the bullets, explosions, and high-speed chases steal the spotlight. After all, those moments are loud, dramatic, and thrilling. But if that's all your story offers, it risks becoming forgettable. What makes a truly gripping action-adventure tale stand out is what's *beneath* the gunfire—the emotional arc of your characters. The inner transformation. The quiet truths unfolding in the chaos. And if you're writing your story in one day, anchoring your action in emotional change will make it feel complete, not just fast.

Think of the action as the canvas, and the emotional journey as the paint. The physical battles mean so much more when they parallel a deeper conflict inside your hero. Are they learning to trust again? Letting go of guilt? Owning their past? Choosing purpose over revenge? A good emotional arc means that who the character is at the start of the story is not who they are at the end—and every explosion, betrayal, or gunfight helped push them toward that change.

Let's start with the **basic shape of an emotional arc**. It usually follows this path: a character starts in a broken, limited, or conflicted state. Through the story's trials, they're forced to face their fears, flaws, or beliefs. Something cracks. They start to shift. By the end, they've grown—or if it's a tragedy, they've failed to grow and paid the price. Now layer that over your action. Ask ChatGPT, "What emotional arc fits a hero who begins as a loner and ends as a selfless leader?" and you've got your internal through-line.

For example, a mercenary who believes in nothing but the paycheck might take a mission that gradually shows him people are worth fighting for. A burned-out agent on one last job might rediscover what it means to *care*. A rookie out for glory might learn that courage means sacrifice. The point is, the action puts pressure on the character's beliefs—and under that pressure, they change.

Every major set piece can serve the emotional arc. A chase scene might not just be about escape—it's the first time the hero puts someone else's safety above their own. A brutal fight might not just be about survival—it's about facing the guilt they've been carrying for years. Ask ChatGPT, "How can a mid-story ambush scene reveal that a character still blames themselves for a past death?" and now your action is *doing emotional work.*

Dialogue, too, can carry this arc—especially in the quiet moments between chaos. A flippant comment early on can turn into a raw confession later. A running joke can die in the final act because the stakes have changed. Ask ChatGPT, "Give me a progression of emotional beats in the relationship between a reluctant hero and their idealistic partner," and you can chart a growing bond through conflict, disagreement, and eventually trust.

One great technique for writing emotionally charged action is to give your characters *triggers*. These are things that dig at the emotional wound—objects, names, smells, locations. Maybe the sight of a burned-out village reminds the hero of one they couldn't save. Maybe a lull in the fighting brings back a memory. Maybe the villain knows the hero's weak spot and keeps pressing it. These little flashes give the story emotional muscle. Ask ChatGPT, "What emotional triggers might haunt a former soldier turned treasure hunter?" and you'll start to see ways to deepen even the most adrenaline-packed sequences.

Another layer to explore is how your characters *handle* emotion. Some bottle it up. Some lash out. Some joke through the pain. This defines how the arc plays out. A stoic hero who finally breaks in the climax—that's powerful. A funny character who suddenly goes silent? That hits. Ask ChatGPT, "How can I show emotional change in a hero who rarely talks about their feelings?" and it'll help you find the subtler beats.

Your villain can—and should—have an emotional arc too. It might be a fall into madness, a descent into obsession, or even a redemption path that gets tragically cut short. The more emotional ground they share with the hero, the more charged their confrontation becomes. Ask ChatGPT, "What's a mirrored emotional arc between a hero and a villain with the same trauma?" and you've got yourself a climax that hits on every level.

Even side characters can carry mini arcs that reinforce or contrast the hero's. The young hothead who learns caution. The mentor figure who finally opens up. The betrayed ally who gets a shot at justice. These emotional subplots make the world feel alive and keep the story from becoming just a string of set pieces. Ask ChatGPT, "Give me an emotional subplot for a sidekick character who starts off resenting the hero," and you'll get dynamic tension you can thread through the narrative.

If you ever feel like your story is sagging in the middle—or your hero is just going through the motions—chances are, it's an emotional issue. Go back to what they want. What they fear. What they're hiding from. Then use the next scene to push on that. Not just with guns, but with stakes. With decisions. With moments that feel like they matter. Ask ChatGPT, "What's a scene that would force my hero to confront their deepest regret while under fire?" and you'll write something that stays with the reader long after the bullets stop flying.

Remember, an emotional arc doesn't have to be a tearful confession or a hug at the end. Sometimes it's as simple as a character who finally stops running. Finally stands up. Finally forgives. Finally believes in something again.

In the end, the explosions are cool—but it's what those explosions *mean* that makes your story unforgettable.

Because what makes your hero compelling isn't that they can shoot, climb, or punch their way out of any trap.

It's that they started out broken, afraid, or lost—and somehow, through the fire, became *more*.

How to Use ChatGPT for Instant Rewrites

One of the best things about writing an action-adventure story in a single day is the momentum. You charge through scenes, ride the adrenaline, and hit all the major beats without second-guessing yourself. But let's be real—when you write fast, some scenes are going to miss. A line of dialogue might fall flat. A fight scene might feel too slow. A twist might land too soft. That's not failure. That's the nature of speed-writing. The magic trick is having a tool like ChatGPT on hand to help you rewrite, rework, and re-energize those weak spots *instantly*.

Think of ChatGPT as your rewrite wingman—the story doctor that never sleeps, never rolls its eyes at another draft, and always has ten ways to fix a problem before your coffee gets cold.

Let's start with dialogue. You've written a scene and it works okay, but the banter isn't snapping. Or the villain's speech sounds like a Bond parody, and not in a good way. That's where you highlight the section and say to ChatGPT: *"Make this dialogue sharper, more natural, and with more tension,"* or *"Rewrite this exchange to show more distrust between the characters."* Boom—you'll get back a cleaned-up version, usually with better rhythm, stronger voice, and more emotion. If it's still not quite right, you say, *"Make it more sarcastic,"* or *"Add a twist of humor but keep the stakes serious."* You're not starting over—you're refining in real time.

Same goes for action scenes. Let's say you've got a rooftop chase, but it feels like it's missing something. You can copy and paste the whole section into ChatGPT and say, *"Rewrite this rooftop chase to add more suspense, sharper pacing, and use of environment,"* and you'll get a version with more punch—possibly with new obstacles, stronger verbs, and smarter reversals. You can then say, *"Make the ending more surprising,"* or *"Have the hero get injured and lose their weapon,"* and now you're not just rewriting—you're upgrading.

Plot twists, too. If you hit a scene and it feels like the twist isn't landing hard enough—or worse, it's predictable—you can say, *"Rewrite this scene with a twist that the reader won't see coming but makes sense in hindsight."* Or even better, *"Give me three alternate twists that would work in this moment but change the stakes."* Within seconds, you're workshopping twists like you've got a writers' room at your fingertips.

Character development? Same deal. Maybe a side character is feeling flat. You wrote them fast, and now they read like a stereotype. You can drop their intro into ChatGPT and say, *"Rewrite this character's introduction to make them feel more complex, with a mysterious past and hidden motive."* Or, *"Add subtle hints in this dialogue that this character is hiding something."* Now your rewrite is doing emotional heavy-lifting, not just fixing typos.

Let's say a scene is too long or slowing the pacing. You don't have to delete it—you can ask ChatGPT, *"Condense this scene without losing its emotional impact or key information."* It'll cut the fat and leave the muscle. Or ask it to *"rewrite this flashback in half the words but keep the tone reflective and tense."* Time saved. Momentum preserved.

Sometimes you'll want to switch tone. Maybe your villain's monologue is too serious and you want it to feel more mocking. Or your final scene is too grim and needs a hopeful note. Ask ChatGPT, *"Rewrite this scene with a darker tone,"* or *"Make this more emotionally uplifting without losing tension."* It's like a tone dial you can turn with your fingertips.

You can also get surgical. *"Rewrite just this one paragraph to build more dread." "Replace this line with something more personal and vulnerable." "Make this fight sequence feel more chaotic and disorienting."* You're not rewriting your whole story—you're refining it, one pulse point at a time.

And here's a fun one—if you're totally unsure about a scene, say: *"What's not working in this paragraph?"* ChatGPT will often give solid critique. It might say the pacing is off, the dialogue is stiff, or the imagery isn't clear. Then you follow up with: *"Fix it."* That's instant feedback loop magic.

Let's say you wrote an ending and it feels flat. You don't want to throw it out—but it needs more fire. Ask ChatGPT, *"Rewrite this ending to feel more earned, with a sense of emotional closure and a final punch."* You'll get a new version. Then you can say, *"Now add a callback to something the hero said earlier,"* and suddenly you've got a tighter, more satisfying resolution.

The real trick is learning to talk to ChatGPT like it's a collaborator. Be specific. Don't just say "make it better." Say, *"Make this character's voice more bitter and ironic,"* or *"Add more visual texture to this chase,"* or *"Give this monologue more subtext about the hero's guilt."* You're not handing over control. You're working together.

And yes—you can even ask for rewrites in different *styles*. Want the scene to feel more cinematic? Ask. Want the dialogue to echo a Tarantino rhythm? Ask. Want a scene to feel like it was written by a '70s pulp novelist with a bad attitude and a bottle of whiskey? Ask. ChatGPT will oblige.

So when the writing hits a wall, don't panic. Don't waste time stuck in your own head. Just run it through ChatGPT, say what you need, and keep the story moving.

Because rewrites don't have to be painful, and they don't have to slow you down.

Not when you've got a creative engine that can reshape your words in seconds.

In a one-day action-adventure story, speed is everything.

And with ChatGPT, rewrites become part of the *momentum*, not the mess.

When to Break the Rules of the Genre

Action-adventure stories come with a well-stocked toolbox. There are rules—unspoken expectations, patterns, and beats—that readers and viewers subconsciously anticipate. We expect the explosive openings, the globe-trotting set pieces, the ticking clocks, the last-second saves, the clear-cut heroes, and the dastardly villains. These familiar genre conventions are what give the action-adventure story its pulse, its style, its swagger. But here's the kicker: every now and then, the most powerful thing you can do is *break those rules*. Not just for the sake of being different—but to surprise, subvert, or deepen the experience. And when you're writing an action-adventure story in a single day, knowing when to break the rules is your secret edge.

The first step is knowing *why* a rule exists. Most genre rules are built around delivering emotional payoff. The hero saves the day. The villain falls. The world is restored. These moments feel good because they fulfill expectations. So when you decide to break one of those patterns, ask yourself: what do I want the audience to feel instead? Shock? Unease? Reflection? Bittersweet catharsis? Because a broken rule is only powerful if it replaces the expected moment with *something stronger*.

Let's talk about one of the biggest rules: **the invincible hero**. In action-adventure, we're used to protagonists who walk away from car crashes, survive explosions, and take down twelve armed guards with a piece of broken furniture. But sometimes, the best move is to *let them lose*. Let them bleed. Let them fail. Or let them walk away from the fight altogether. That choice can say more about who they are than any victory ever could. You can ask ChatGPT, "What's a powerful way for a hero to fail their mission but still grow emotionally?" and you'll get story beats that sting—in the best way.

Another classic rule: **the happy ending**. Usually, we want the world saved, the bad guys punished, the hero rewarded. But some stories hit harder when the ending is messy. Maybe the villain gets away. Maybe the hero has to sacrifice something enormous. Maybe peace is restored, but at a cost that leaves everyone a little broken. Ask ChatGPT, "What are examples of emotionally resonant endings in action-adventure stories that aren't traditional victories?" and you'll find ways to land your story with weight instead of just noise.

Here's a bold move: **don't open with action**. Wait—what? In action-adventure? Hear me out. Starting with a quiet, intimate, or emotionally charged moment can make the eventual chaos feel even more intense. If you open with a slow-burn mystery or a subtle betrayal, you build *suspense*. Then, when the action does hit, it hits *harder*. Ask ChatGPT, "How can I open an action-adventure story with emotional tension instead of physical danger?" and you'll craft a hook that surprises and seduces instead of just slamming the gas pedal.

Let's talk **villains**. The rule says your antagonist must be powerful, evil, and clearly opposed to the hero's goals. But what if the antagonist is right? What if they're doing the wrong thing for the right reasons? Or what if they're trying to save the world in their own twisted way—and the hero starts to question if they're on the right side? Subverting the villain archetype adds complexity to the conflict. Ask ChatGPT, "What's a morally complex antagonist that forces the hero to question their mission?" and you'll suddenly have conflict that hits harder than any car chase.

You can even play with **genre fusion**. Mix in elements from mystery, horror, sci-fi, or even romance. Let an action-adventure plot play out like a psychological thriller. Or tell the story out of order, start with the ending, or use unreliable narration. Ask ChatGPT, "How can I fuse noir storytelling into a jungle treasure-hunt action story?" and the rules of one genre can be used to flip the expectations of another.

Dialogue is another place to break the mold. Action-adventure is known for quips, one-liners, and punchy banter. But sometimes silence speaks louder. Let the characters *not* say what they're feeling. Let a moment stretch with discomfort. Let someone respond to a heartfelt question with a glance or a shrug instead of a witty comeback. Ask ChatGPT, "Write a silent exchange between two former allies after a betrayal," and you'll see how stillness and subtext can hit harder than words.

And one of the most effective rule-breaking techniques? **The unexpected death.** Killing off a major character mid-story breaks the rules in a way that changes everything. It's a gut punch—but if done right, it propels the story into deeper emotional territory. Ask ChatGPT, "How can I kill off a major character in an action story in a way that deepens the theme?" and you'll find ways to turn tragedy into transformation.

You don't need to break every rule. In fact, if you do, the story loses shape. But picking the *right* rule to break at the right moment can elevate your entire narrative. It's like a guitar solo that goes just slightly off-key—and suddenly, the audience leans in, unsure what's coming next.

So when you're blasting through your action-adventure story in one day and you hit a scene that feels too familiar, too easy, or too clean—pause.

And ask: *What if I did the opposite of what's expected?*

Then let ChatGPT help you reshape the moment.

Because sometimes the best way to honor a genre...

Is to break it wide open.

Writing Chapters like Cliffhangers

If you want your action-adventure story to feel like a pulse-pounding, can't-look-away thrill ride, then every chapter you write should end like the reader just slipped off the edge of a cliff. That's the whole point of a cliffhanger—it keeps the reader turning pages. And when you're writing a full story in a single day, that sense of momentum becomes your best friend. The cliffhanger is the trick that pulls the reader out of the paragraph and into the next scene before they even realize they've crossed a chapter break.

The mistake a lot of writers make is thinking that a cliffhanger always has to be a life-or-death moment. It doesn't. Sometimes it's a literal cliff—a dangling rope, a plummeting vehicle, a collapsing floor. But other times, the cliffhanger is emotional, psychological, or even moral. It's a question left hanging. A line of dialogue cut short. A door that opens without showing us who's behind it. The art is in *what you leave unresolved*—and how urgently the reader needs to find out what happens next.

Let's say you're writing an action sequence. The hero's trying to outrun an avalanche, and the chapter ends just as they leap toward a ledge. That's classic. But what if the cliffhanger was subtler? What if the hero escapes the avalanche but finds a strange symbol carved into the rock—one they recognize from their past? That opens a whole new door. Ask ChatGPT, "Give me subtle cliffhanger moments that don't involve physical danger," and you'll get options that build mystery, tension, and forward motion without explosions.

Here's the real key: every chapter should *create a new question*. Not necessarily a huge one—but something the reader needs answered. What's in the briefcase? Who just fired the shot? Why did the ally suddenly go quiet? What did the villain mean by "You'll thank me later"? These don't need to be big plot twists. They just need to trigger curiosity. Ask ChatGPT, "What kind of unresolved question can I end a jungle exploration chapter with?" and you'll get ideas that tie directly to your setting and tone.

Let's talk structure. Ending a chapter on a cliffhanger doesn't mean you cut the scene short at a random place. It means you *build up to a break in tension*—and then refuse to resolve it until the next chapter. You wind the scene tighter, tighter, tighter... and then snap the thread. End right before the answer. Before the punch. Before the betrayal. Before the kiss. Before the realization. It doesn't have to be a shock—it just has to be *unfinished*. ChatGPT can help you with this pacing trick. Ask, "How can I restructure this chapter to end on a beat that creates suspense or intrigue?" and you'll get a smarter ending without starting over.

One underrated move is the **double cliffhanger**—ending a chapter with one problem, and beginning the next with *another*. The hero gets out of the trap—but into a worse one. The betrayal is revealed—but so is a deeper conspiracy. The clue is found—but the person who can explain it is already dead. This constant shifting of pressure keeps the reader just off-balance enough to stay hooked. You can say to ChatGPT, "Give me a double cliffhanger sequence for a character escaping from a lab," and get a rapid-fire chain of problems to build on.

You can also end a chapter with a moment of realization. Not action. Not dialogue. Just a single, quiet thought that reframes everything. The kind of line that gives the reader chills and makes them *need* to know what the character does next. A good example might be: "It wasn't the first time she'd seen that scar." Or, "He wasn't running from the enemy. He was running from what he left behind." These soft cliffhangers have *teeth*. Ask ChatGPT, "Give me closing lines that turn a quiet scene into a cliffhanger," and you'll get those quiet gut-punches that make the next chapter inevitable.

Another fun trick is to **end in motion**. Don't tie up the action neatly—cut the chapter mid-movement. Mid-fall. Mid-decision. The reader doesn't get to rest—they get swept along. A chapter that ends with, "He pulled the trigger," or "She stepped into the darkness," or "They turned the corner—and stopped," leaves just enough unresolved detail that the brain fills in the gap with anticipation. That's the secret: you're not giving answers—you're giving *urgency*.

And don't forget dialogue cliffhangers. These are some of the easiest and most effective ways to keep things tense. Let someone say something shocking and end the chapter before the reply. Or drop a name, a threat, a promise—then cut to black. Ask ChatGPT, "Write five chapter-ending lines of dialogue that raise the stakes," and you'll find endings that snap like a whip.

When writing a full story in one day, this technique is more than just style—it's survival. Cliffhangers keep *you* moving as much as the reader. They make your writing addictive. You finish one chapter already excited to start the next. They stop you from meandering, because you're always pushing toward that hook, that beat, that moment of suspense.

You don't need to write like you're ending every chapter on a Hollywood commercial break—but you *do* want each chapter to feel like the story just turned a corner.

So if you ever find yourself asking, "Is this the end of the chapter?"—make sure the next sentence is something your reader *can't* walk away from.

And if it isn't?

Hand it to ChatGPT and say:

"Make this end like everything depends on what happens next."

Because in action-adventure, it kind of does.

Integrating Mystery into the Mayhem

One of the most satisfying moves you can pull in an action-adventure story is slipping a mystery right into the middle of the chaos. Explosions are fun, sure. Chase scenes? Always. But when you layer a puzzle under the punches, suddenly your audience isn't just holding on for the thrills—they're leaning in, trying to figure things out. And when you're writing your story in a single day, adding mystery can be the glue that holds everything together. It gives your action scenes a *reason*. It gives your characters *purpose*. It gives your audience a hook that doesn't rely on gunfire or freefalls.

Mystery doesn't mean slowing things down. It means raising questions faster than you answer them. It means revealing that the stolen briefcase isn't just full of money—it's full of *blueprints*. It means that the bad guys aren't chasing the hero just for revenge—they want something they think the hero knows, but maybe *doesn't*. The mystery adds layers to the mayhem. Every fight might solve a clue. Every chase might uncover a secret. Every near-death escape might lead to a revelation that twists the story deeper.

So where do you start? With a single unanswered question. That's all it takes to hook both the reader and the characters. A strange symbol on a wall. A name whispered in the last breath of an informant. A missing file. A betrayal that doesn't add up. You plant the question early—then chase the answer across the whole story. Ask ChatGPT, "What's a simple mystery I can introduce in the first scene of an action story?" and you'll get questions that can be unraveled in layers as your story blasts forward.

The best mysteries in action-adventure are physical. You can *touch* them. A strange artifact. A bloodstained map. A phone with encrypted messages. A scar on the villain's neck that the hero recognizes. These aren't just puzzles—they're *clues*. And they lead somewhere, even if no one knows where yet. That gives your characters a reason to move. Ask ChatGPT, "What are five physical clues a hero might find in an abandoned embassy that hint at a deeper conspiracy?" and your mystery practically starts writing itself.

Let's talk structure. As you're racing through the plot, you can use mystery to break up the action beats and add rhythm. It goes like this: *action → discovery → suspicion → action*. You're not just running from bad guys—you're running because you just found something that changes everything. That piece of paper you pulled from the burning wreckage? It's got coordinates. That fight in the stairwell? It ends with the villain shouting, "She knows the truth!" Now your characters aren't just reacting—they're *investigating*, even as the world explodes around them.

Mystery also gives your characters layers. The hero isn't just brave—they're *curious*. They're chasing answers, not just safety. Maybe they're piecing together a hidden past. Maybe they're trying to figure out who betrayed them. Maybe the person they thought was a sidekick is actually working for the enemy. Ask ChatGPT, "How can I build a mystery subplot around a hero who doesn't remember parts of their last mission?" and you'll turn the hero's mind into part of the battleground.

And villains? They become way more compelling when they're part of a mystery. Maybe they're not who they say they are. Maybe they're hunting something ancient, or covering up something monstrous. Maybe the villain isn't even the real antagonist. Use mystery to blur the lines. Ask ChatGPT, "What's a twist reveal that makes the villain a pawn in someone else's plan?" and you'll keep the tension tight right until the final act.

Mystery thrives on *information control*. Let the audience know *almost* enough. Give them puzzle pieces, but not the whole picture. Use overheard conversations. Mysterious files. Recovered footage. Half-burned letters. Keep dropping breadcrumbs. Then use action scenes to interrupt every answer. Just when the hero's about to figure it out—BOOM.

Gunfire. Explosion. Helicopter crash. It's not just mayhem for the sake of spectacle—it's conflict *designed* to keep the truth buried just a little longer.

Another powerful trick? Flashback clues. The hero sees or hears something in the present that triggers a memory—and the past reveals a piece of the puzzle. But never dump the whole truth at once. Let the flashbacks raise new questions even as they answer old ones. Ask ChatGPT, "Write a flashback scene that reveals part of a secret without explaining everything," and you'll get a scene that deepens the story instead of slowing it.

Let your settings reflect the mystery. Ancient ruins with warnings carved in stone. Secret bunkers filled with files no one's supposed to read. A storm-battered town where no one talks about the night the fire happened. Locations become characters in the mystery—and every environment your hero enters should offer either a clue or a complication. Ask ChatGPT, "Describe a mystery-filled setting for an action scene in a forgotten underground train station," and you'll be writing your next chapter before you even realize it.

And yes—mystery also fuels *twists*. You can use red herrings to send the hero chasing the wrong goal. You can drop false allies into their path. You can build a mystery so compelling that the final reveal hits like a truck. Not because it was shocking—but because everything secretly pointed to it. Ask ChatGPT, "What's a twist that reframes an earlier scene without breaking continuity?" and you'll turn your plot into a maze with a beating heart.

So the next time you're in the middle of a gunfight or a high-speed chase, ask yourself—what else can be *happening* here? What's being hidden? What's being revealed? What clue is falling out of someone's pocket, unnoticed?

Because when you layer mystery into the mayhem, your story doesn't just move—it *pulls*.

It becomes a puzzle wrapped in a firestorm. And the only way out...

Is to chase the truth all the way through the chaos.

Combining Action and Adventure with Comedy

There's a special kind of storytelling magic that happens when you throw adrenaline and absurdity into the same blender. When punches are being thrown, traps are being triggered, and someone still has the nerve to crack a joke or roll their eyes mid-explosion—that's when action-adventure and comedy collide. It's a delicate balance, but when done right, it's unforgettable. You get stories that are thrilling *and* ridiculous, characters who are tough but witty, and moments of high tension that snap into laughter without killing the stakes. Think *Indiana Jones*, *The Mummy*, *Guardians of the Galaxy*, or *21 Jump Street*. These aren't just fun action stories—they're comic rollercoasters that never stop moving.

So how do you write something that kicks ass *and* cracks up the reader—especially when you're writing your action-adventure story in a single day? You build rhythm. You know when to play it straight, when to lean into chaos, and when to drop the perfect line just as things go sideways.

Let's start with the golden rule: **comedy doesn't kill tension—it *releases* it.** Action builds pressure. The chase, the fight, the ticking bomb. And then, right at the edge, a well-placed joke lets the audience breathe. Not in a way that weakens the moment—but in a way that makes the tension even *sharper* when it comes back. A sarcastic one-liner during a shootout doesn't ruin the danger—it makes the characters feel *human*. Ask ChatGPT, "Give me five one-liners a hero might say during a chaotic car chase," and you'll be punching up the scene without deflating the stakes.

Timing is everything. The comedy works best when it cuts *against* the intensity. A quiet, emotional moment? Maybe not the place for a pratfall. But a firefight in a kitchen? Yeah, a character throwing a frying pan in self-defense absolutely works. You can let the environment play into the comedy. Ask ChatGPT, "What's a funny way a hero could win a fight using only objects found in a supermarket?" and you'll get scenes that are equal parts badass and ridiculous.

Characters are your comedy engines. If one of them is a walking disaster, or never knows when to shut up, or insists on being upbeat in the middle of carnage—they can deliver laughs just by being themselves. You don't need a punchline every page. You just need characters whose personalities naturally cause friction. The straight-laced hero and the mouthy sidekick. The sarcastic ex-spy and the overly sincere intern. Ask ChatGPT, "Create a dynamic between two action heroes who have completely opposite personalities," and you'll instantly have comedy built into every scene.

But here's the thing—**you don't want your comedy to make the characters seem dumb unless that's the point.** Smart characters doing stupid things on purpose can be hilarious. Smart characters doing dumb things *accidentally* can be charming. But if they're just stumbling through the plot with no agency, the story loses power. Keep the characters sharp. Let them be funny because they're *aware* of the absurdity around them—not because they're clowns.

Another great trick is **repeating gags**. Something that starts off as a joke in Act One comes back in Act Three during a huge set piece and becomes part of the action. Maybe the hero keeps saying, "I hate ladders." They say it again as they tumble down a stairwell during a fight. And then, at the climax, they have to climb a rickety ladder over a pit of fire—and mutter the line one last time before the big leap. That callback hits *because* it's been earned. Ask ChatGPT, "What's a running joke that could tie into a major set-piece in an action-comedy story?" and let it become a rhythm the audience looks forward to.

Let the *failures* be funny. Your hero tries to be cool and slips on a banana peel. The villain delivers a long speech and forgets their own plan. The hero dramatically disarms a bomb—then realizes it wasn't even armed. These moments are funny because they *feel real* in a world where everything is usually so slick and perfect. Ask ChatGPT, "Write a comedic failure that still moves the action forward," and you'll see how laughs and progress can go hand-in-hand.

The comedy can also be **verbal**—banter, sarcasm, arguments in the middle of chaos. Two characters yelling at each other about directions while under fire. A villain annoyed that no one takes his monologue seriously. A side character who insists on explaining a complex plan *during* a prison break. Ask ChatGPT, "Give me dialogue where two characters argue about their plan during a chase," and suddenly the scene is doing double duty—building tension and cracking smiles.

Even quiet comedy has a place. Maybe the hero sits in silence after a massive shootout and mutters, "Well, that went *almost* according to plan." Maybe a dog steals the key in the middle of a tense standoff. Maybe the villain is fuming while classical music plays in the background. Comedy in these moments makes the characters relatable, the scenes memorable, and the pace electric.

Just make sure the emotional core of the story isn't undercut. If there's loss, if there's pain—let it breathe. Let the characters feel it. Comedy is the pressure valve, not the escape hatch. You can follow up a tragic moment with something awkward or oddly funny to *contrast* the mood—but don't erase the impact. Ask ChatGPT, "How can I follow a character's emotional low point with a moment of lightness that doesn't cheapen the emotion?" and you'll keep the tone balanced.

Remember, action-adventure and comedy thrive on *momentum*. You want scenes that race forward *and* surprise. That hit hard *and* land a laugh. It's a rhythm—tense, funny, tense, funny, then BAM—twist, punch, revelation.

When it works, you get characters who are brave but sarcastic, vulnerable but sharp, and moments that are both edge-of-your-seat and laugh-out-loud. And when you're writing the whole thing in a day, letting the comedy flow naturally through the action makes the process more fun—and your story more alive.

Because the best kind of action is thrilling.

And the best kind of comedy is the kind that kicks down the door.

Put them together?

You've got a story that *never* stops entertaining.

Romance on the Run: Love in High Stakes

There's something electric about love in the middle of danger. When two characters are dodging bullets, leaping off trains, or racing through enemy territory, the stakes of their relationship rise with every heartbeat. It's not just about sparks flying—it's about connection forged in the crucible of chaos. In action-adventure stories, romance doesn't slow things down. When done right, it *amplifies* everything. It deepens the risk, raises the stakes, and gives every explosive moment a human core. And when you're writing your action-adventure story in a single day, weaving a romantic thread through the madness can be exactly what keeps your audience hooked emotionally, not just viscerally.

First things first—**romance in action stories works best when it's earned through survival, not sweetness.** These characters aren't sitting on picnic blankets or whispering in candlelight. They're bleeding, sweating, shouting, hiding, rescuing each other, and sometimes arguing in the middle of life-or-death decisions. Love under pressure is about trust, adrenaline, and unexpected vulnerability. It doesn't have to be tender—it has to *mean something*. Ask ChatGPT, "Give me ways two characters can fall for each other while under constant threat," and you'll get moments of connection that feel raw and believable.

The setup matters. You don't need your characters to start with googly eyes. In fact, opposites clashing can be a goldmine. Maybe they're from different worlds—a rogue and a soldier, a scientist and a smuggler, a cop and a thief. Maybe they don't trust each other at first. Maybe they even *despise* each other. That tension creates friction—and friction creates sparks. Ask ChatGPT, "What's a strong setup for two action heroes who can't stand each other but are forced to work together?" and you'll be halfway to fireworks already.

The most believable action-adventure romances unfold through *moments of rescue, risk, and revelation*. One character helps the other when they're wounded. They argue about a plan, but the fight is really about fear. They think the other is lost—only to be reunited, changed, shaken, and closer than ever. These beats don't need to pause the action—they *are* the action. They unfold *through* the conflict. Ask ChatGPT, "How can I show romantic tension during a mission gone wrong?" and your scene will do double duty—delivering both danger and desire.

One powerful trick is to let the romance reveal the characters' **emotional core**. Action shows what they can do. Love shows who they are. Maybe the confident mercenary shows fear only when the person they care about is threatened. Maybe the calculating strategist starts taking reckless risks because they can't bear to lose the one person who sees through them. These shifts show vulnerability in high-stakes moments. And that vulnerability is what turns attraction into something real. Ask ChatGPT, "What's a scene where a hardened hero finally admits they care, but only under duress?" and you'll find your emotional turning point.

You can play the long game, too. A slow-burn romance unfolding over the course of your action-adventure story adds layers. Each close call brings them a little closer. Each disagreement chips away at their walls. Each victory or loss is shared. And when the kiss finally happens—or the hand touch, or the admission, or the look—it *lands*. Not because it's romantic on its own, but because of what they've survived together. Ask ChatGPT, "What are small romantic beats that can be woven into an action-heavy story without disrupting the pace?" and you'll have the tools to thread emotion through the explosions.

Humor works, too. Banter is one of the best romantic weapons in action-adventure. It builds rapport, reveals character, and lightens the tension just enough to make the serious moments hit harder. Let them tease each other, argue about who saved who, trade insults that turn into grins. Ask ChatGPT, "Write a flirty but sarcastic exchange between two characters while escaping enemy fire," and you'll feel the rhythm of love-on-the-run.

Now let's talk intimacy. Not just physical, but emotional. You can have a powerful romantic beat in a single glance, a shared memory, a silent moment between chaos. These don't take up time—they add *meaning* to time. They remind the reader that beneath the fire and fury, something human is happening. Something real. Something worth fighting for.

And if you really want the romance to matter—**make it cost something.** Maybe their feelings get in the way. Maybe one has to choose between saving the other and completing the mission. Maybe one is captured and the other risks it all to get them back. Let the love *raise the stakes*, not lower them. Because once your hero has something to lose, every moment becomes more fragile. More urgent. More *alive*. Ask ChatGPT, "How can romance raise the emotional tension in a climactic action scene?" and you'll find a way to thread love into the final blow.

Sometimes the best endings don't wrap the romance up neatly. Maybe they part ways. Maybe one doesn't make it. Or maybe, at the end of it all, they finally sit down, laugh through their bruises, and realize—*that was insane... but maybe it was the start of something real.* Ask ChatGPT, "Write a bittersweet but hopeful ending for two action-adventure characters who've just survived hell together," and you'll close on a note that's earned, honest, and unforgettable.

Because romance on the run isn't about grand gestures.

It's about eye contact across a battlefield.

A hand that doesn't let go.

A breathless moment between explosions where two people realize they're not alone.

That's the kind of love that makes the stakes matter.

That's the kind of love worth running toward.

Creating Legendary Heroes with ChatGPT

In the world of action-adventure, heroes are more than just people who fight and survive—they become *icons*. The best of them don't just shoot straight and punch hard; they leave an imprint on readers and viewers that lasts long after the story ends. They stand for something. They have *presence*. Whether it's Indiana Jones with his hat and whip, Lara Croft with her dual pistols and daring, or Ethan Hunt scaling skyscrapers with raw determination, legendary heroes feel larger than life—*but* they're always rooted in something deeply human. And the great news is, when you're writing your action-adventure story in one day, you don't have to create that legend alone. You've got ChatGPT at your side.

Creating a legendary hero starts with **distinction**. Who are they? What do they do that no one else does? What do they *believe* in when everything goes to hell? You want a personality that can punch through the noise. They don't have to be perfect—but they need to stand for something. Maybe they always protect the innocent. Maybe they never leave a teammate behind. Maybe they're haunted by a past mistake they're trying to redeem. Ask ChatGPT, "Help me design a morally complex hero with a clear personal code," and you'll get a blueprint for someone unforgettable.

Next, dig into the **visual and behavioral signatures**. Think about your hero's look, their gear, their habits. James Bond doesn't just fight—he drinks martinis a certain way. Mad Max doesn't just drive—he broods like the apocalypse owes him something. Your hero needs traits, quirks, and tools that set them apart. These are the things fans remember, the things that define them in a single frame or sentence. Ask ChatGPT, "What are five signature traits that would make my hero instantly recognizable?" and now you're sculpting identity, not just role.

Every legendary hero also has a **backstory that burns**. Even if you don't reveal it all up front, it should be there—shaping the way they talk, fight, trust, and decide. Were they betrayed? Exiled? Once on the wrong side of the fight? Did they lose someone, fail to save someone, or walk away from something they believed in? These experiences *shape* their choices in the now. You can say to ChatGPT, "Give me a tragic backstory for a hero who never talks about their past but acts like it controls them," and you'll get emotional fuel for every action beat.

But here's what really sets legends apart—they have **internal conflict**. Not just external problems, but *emotional weight*. Maybe they hate violence but are forced into it. Maybe they want to be left alone but keep being pulled back in. Maybe they don't believe they're the good guy anymore, even when everyone else does. These conflicts give them *depth*. They let readers and viewers connect to someone who otherwise might seem too superhuman to care about. Ask ChatGPT, "What internal struggle would add emotional depth to a high-functioning action hero?" and suddenly you've got more than a fighter—you've got a soul.

Now think about their **relationships**. Legendary heroes never stand alone. They clash with mentors, protect sidekicks, lose allies, fall in love and betray or get betrayed. How they connect—or refuse to connect—matters. Let their heroism be *seen* through others' eyes. Maybe someone worships them. Maybe someone resents them. Maybe someone loves them, but they keep pushing away. Ask ChatGPT, "How can I show my hero's growth through their changing relationships with their team?" and you'll create emotional arcs that echo through the action.

A legendary hero also needs **a cause that transcends them**. They're not just doing this for money, thrills, or revenge (even if that's how it starts). Eventually, they're fighting for something *bigger*. Maybe they become the only one willing to do the right thing. Maybe they stand between total chaos and a sliver of order. That doesn't mean they preach—it means their *actions* define them. Ask ChatGPT, "What's a cause or belief my hero could embody without turning into a cliché?" and you'll uncover deeper purpose.

And then there's the **moment of choice**. All great heroes face a scene where they have to decide: sacrifice comfort for duty, safety for truth, self-interest for someone else. These are the turning points that *make* legends. When the hero refuses to run. When they go back for someone. When they take the hard path, knowing what it'll cost. These are the moments audiences remember. Ask ChatGPT, "What's a powerful decision my hero could make that defines who they really are?" and you'll have your story's spine.

Let's not forget that even legendary heroes need to **fail sometimes**. Maybe they fall for a trap. Maybe they make a mistake. Maybe they lose something or someone important. The fall makes the rise more powerful. A perfect hero isn't inspiring—they're boring. But a wounded hero who still stands up? That's what makes people cheer. Ask ChatGPT, "Describe a believable failure that tests a hero's resolve without destroying their likability," and you'll strike the perfect balance between strength and humanity.

Want to fast-track your process? Ask ChatGPT to build you a full hero profile:

"Create a legendary action-adventure protagonist with a unique skill set, emotional wound, and signature style."

You'll get a ready-to-use character that you can customize, refine, and drop right into your story.

The best part? You don't need to get it perfect on the first try. You can bounce back and forth—"Now make them funnier," or "Give them a darker flaw," or "What's a catchphrase that fits this character's vibe?" You can iterate in minutes what would normally take days.

Because with the right vision and the right prompts, ChatGPT becomes your co-creator, helping you sculpt a hero who feels like they walked out of a legend and straight into the line of fire.

And when they finally step onto the page—scarred, driven, unrelenting, unforgettable—you'll know you didn't just create a protagonist.

You created a *myth*.

A name readers will remember.

A presence that fills every scene.

A hero that deserves the spotlight—

and *owns* it.

Research Fast: Let ChatGPT Do the Heavy Lifting

One of the biggest time-killers when writing any story—especially something grounded in danger, combat, history, or exotic locations—is research. You open one tab to look up how satellite phones work, and suddenly it's an hour later and you're knee-deep in articles about Cold War espionage. That rabbit hole might be interesting, but it doesn't help you *finish the story*. And when you're trying to write a complete action-adventure tale in a single day, research can feel like an anchor dragging you down. That's why the smartest move is to let ChatGPT carry the load for you.

Think of it like this: you're the director calling the shots, and ChatGPT is your production crew, research assistant, and location scout rolled into one. The key isn't just knowing that it *can* research for you—it's knowing *how* to ask so you get exactly what you need, fast.

Let's say your hero is breaking into a high-security vault. You don't have time to read three hours of white papers on security systems. Just ask ChatGPT, "What kind of modern security features would a high-tech vault have, and how could someone realistically bypass them in a story?" In seconds, you'll get a streamlined explanation of infrared sensors, biometric locks, motion detection, and plausible ways around them. Not only is it faster—it's *story-ready*. You're not just learning facts. You're getting tools to build drama.

Need a setting? Ask, "What are some remote and visually striking locations in South America that could be used for a hidden research lab?" You'll get a list of jungle canopies, ancient ruins, storm-swept cliffs, and maybe even a forgotten salt flat. Then follow up with, "What kind of wildlife or weather conditions would make this location more dangerous?" and suddenly your setting becomes a source of conflict and atmosphere.

Writing a fight scene and need the right move? Ask, "What's a believable but unexpected martial arts technique that could disarm an opponent with a knife?" Boom—your action just got smarter, and you didn't have to lose an hour to YouTube tutorials.

Trying to figure out how long it takes to hack a secure network? Just ask. Need to know what kind of injuries a character might suffer in a car crash and still keep going? Ask. Want to make sure your villain's plan to poison a water supply doesn't sound completely ridiculous? Ask.

Here's the real power move: don't just ask for facts. Ask for *story context*. Instead of saying "What is the history of the Panama Canal?", ask, "How could the Panama Canal be used as the backdrop for an action-adventure scene involving sabotage and a cover-up?" Now the answer comes loaded with *ideas*, not just information.

You can also get ChatGPT to **simulate knowledge from character perspectives**. Let's say your character is a former CIA analyst. Ask, "Write a short paragraph explaining how satellite tracking works, as if a retired CIA agent is explaining it to someone who's never heard of it." Now you've got technical exposition dressed up in character voice, ready for your story.

When you're building gear, gadgets, or tech-based plot devices, you don't need blueprints. You need *believability*. Ask ChatGPT, "Create a believable prototype for a portable EMP device a rogue agent might use," and you'll get something that sounds just real enough to sell the scene.

And when you're worldbuilding—especially for historical or sci-fi adventure stories—you can ask ChatGPT to *fill in the gaps*. "What are some ancient codes that might be used in a lost scroll?" or "Describe a plausible political crisis in a fictional Eastern European country that could justify foreign intervention." You're not writing a textbook. You're writing fiction. You just need something that sounds *true enough* to let the story fly.

Another major time-saver? **Dialogue coaching.** If your characters need to argue about a historical fact, a cultural reference, or a tactical decision, just say, "Write a short argument between a hotheaded soldier and a cool-headed scientist about the ethics of detonating an experimental device in a civilian area." Now the scene doesn't just *move*—it *educates*, all without you pausing to learn everything about blast radii or battlefield ethics.

You can also use ChatGPT to cross-check your assumptions. If you write a scene where someone jumps from a helicopter into the ocean, you might pause and wonder, "Could they actually survive that?" Instead of digging through survival blogs, just ask, "What would happen if someone jumped into deep ocean water from 100 feet up? How would you survive it in a story?" You'll get the answer—plus a better version of the scene, grounded in logic but pumped full of tension.

And sometimes, you just need a name. For a city. A piece of ancient tech. A secret organization. Instead of staring into space for twenty minutes, ask, "Give me ten cool-sounding names for an underground criminal syndicate with ties to ancient relics," and you'll be spoiled for choice.

The point is, when you use ChatGPT for research, you're not cutting corners—you're *clearing the path*. You're reducing friction so the story can flow. You're spending more time in your creative zone and less time swimming through unrelated search results. You're turning the endless info-mess of the internet into a fast, focused, custom-tailored writer's toolkit.

And when you're racing the clock, trying to get a full story down in one epic day, that speed makes all the difference.

So the next time your plot gets technical, or your characters enter unknown terrain, or you hit a wall of "I don't know how this works," don't stall out.

Just say:

"Hey ChatGPT—do the heavy lifting."

And watch the answers come flying in like backup on a black ops mission.

From the Amazon to Atlantis: Building Fictional Worlds

One of the joys of writing action-adventure stories is that you're not stuck in one place—you get to go everywhere. Your characters can leap from the Amazon rainforest to a secret Antarctic outpost, race through ancient temples in Cambodia, dive into sunken cities, or uncover hidden fortresses carved into Himalayan cliffs. And if those places don't exist? No problem. You can invent them. When you're writing an action-adventure tale in a single day, building fictional worlds—or blending the real with the imagined—is not only possible, it's one of the fastest ways to add excitement, scale, and mystery to your story.

Worldbuilding in action-adventure isn't just about location—it's about *the experience*. Where are the characters standing? What do they see, hear, smell, and fear? What's lurking just out of sight? And more importantly—what makes this place feel *bigger than the moment they're in*? You want your world to feel alive, dangerous, and packed with story waiting to happen.

Let's start with the **real places twisted with a fictional edge**. You don't need to invent everything from scratch. Take the Amazon. It's massive, wild, and full of secrets. But what if, deep in an uncharted pocket of rainforest, there's a pre-human ruin with carvings that don't match any known civilization? Suddenly the real world becomes the launchpad for myth. Ask ChatGPT, "What could be hidden deep in the Amazon that no one has discovered—something fictional but grounded in real history?" and you'll get ideas that walk the line between believable and fantastical.

Then there's **Atlantis-style worldbuilding**—fully fictional settings with their own history, rules, dangers, and culture. These places are perfect for adding mystery and myth to your action. Think of cities buried beneath the sea, temples that move when no one's looking, or entire regions erased from maps by governments that fear what's buried there. Ask ChatGPT, "Create a lost city hidden beneath the Sahara with ancient traps and a secret that could change the world," and you'll get everything from visuals to legend to potential conflict—all ready to weave into your narrative.

When building your world quickly, focus on **purpose-driven design**. You don't need to draw maps or write history books. Just ask: What's the function of this place in the story? Is it a trap? A sanctuary? A final battleground? A place where something sacred is hidden? Let that guide the details. A vault designed to protect a weapon looks and feels different than one meant to keep people *out*. Ask ChatGPT, "Describe the interior of a forgotten war bunker that's now guarding a lost artifact," and it'll drop you right into the atmosphere.

Also, don't forget to layer your world with **clues and consequences**. Every place your characters go should feel like it's been touched by time. Scratched walls. Overgrown statues. Rotting documents. Symbols. Murals. Clues left behind. Each location should move the story forward. You don't want your characters wandering through pretty scenery—you want them uncovering things, triggering traps, finding out too late that something they saw earlier mattered. Ask ChatGPT, "What small environmental details could hint at danger in an abandoned jungle research facility?" and suddenly the world is *talking* to the characters.

Weather and terrain also matter in worldbuilding. The snowstorm that cuts off escape. The monsoon that turns dirt into a trap. The desert heat that turns a chase into a death march. These aren't just background—they *are* the challenge. Ask ChatGPT, "How can I use terrain to make an action scene in a canyon more intense?" and your environment becomes a character in its own right.

And then there's **culture and legend**. If your fictional world once belonged to a lost civilization, or is currently inhabited by people guarding secrets, you'll want to sprinkle in just enough to give it depth. Beliefs, rituals, taboos, even the way locals look at your characters can all raise the tension. They're not just visiting a place—they're trespassing on something ancient, sacred, or cursed. Ask ChatGPT, "Create a local legend that warns travelers away from a mountain that hides an ancient weapon," and now your setting comes with *warning signs* and *mystique*.

If your story jumps between multiple settings—as many action-adventures do—make sure each one feels distinct. The jungle shouldn't feel like the city. The desert shouldn't feel like the arctic. You want sensory contrast. Use different colors, light, sounds, architecture, climate, wildlife. Ask ChatGPT, "Help me describe three contrasting global locations for an action-adventure story involving a global treasure hunt," and you'll get enough contrast to keep the audience fully immersed.

And remember: **don't over explain**. Let the mystery breathe. Sometimes it's scarier when the ruins are unexplained, when the markings can't be translated, when the layout of the labyrinth doesn't make sense. The unknown is your ally. Readers want to wonder what else might be hiding beneath the surface. Ask ChatGPT, "How can I create a setting that feels ancient and unknowable, without dumping exposition?" and you'll get elegant ways to suggest history without slowing the pace.

When you're moving fast, ChatGPT can even build full environments for you on the fly. Try:

"Describe a booby-trapped underground temple with ancient technology and supernatural elements."

Or:

"Create a floating island in a hidden part of the ocean protected by electromagnetic storms and cloaked by myth."

In seconds, you'll get structure, purpose, visual flair, and sensory detail.

That's the power of combining action-adventure storytelling with AI worldbuilding—you don't have to slow down to make it rich. You don't need to map out everything. You just need the place to *feel real enough to kill someone*, *save someone*, or *change someone*. And ChatGPT can feed you vivid details while you keep your fingers on the keyboard and the story moving forward.

Because whether your hero is deep in the Amazon, lost beneath Atlantis, or climbing a rope ladder into a cursed temple in the clouds, it's not just about where they go.

It's about where they're *pulled*—by danger, by wonder, and by the thrill of finding something no one was meant to find.

And in a one-day writing sprint, that's the kind of world that writes *itself*.

Making the Adventure Matter: Stakes beyond Survival

Action-adventure stories are loaded with peril. Your hero's dangling from a cliff, outnumbered in a shootout, racing against a clock, dodging lasers, or jumping from a moving vehicle. But if all the audience cares about is whether the hero lives or dies, you're only scratching the surface of what action-adventure can be. Survival is the bare minimum. The *real* power of this genre comes when the story stakes reach beyond just staying alive. It's when what's at risk is emotional, moral, ideological, or deeply personal. That's when an adventure stops being just exciting—and starts to *matter*.

Let's start with a question: *What does your hero stand to lose if they fail—besides their own life?* This could be someone they love. A city. A community. A legacy. An ideal. Their own integrity. The best action-adventure stories aren't about avoiding death—they're about *protecting something more important than themselves*. Think about Indiana Jones in *The Last Crusade* choosing to let the Grail go to save his father. Or *The Dark Knight*, where Batman chooses to take the fall to protect Gotham's hope. Or *Mad Max: Fury Road*, where survival becomes secondary to liberating the oppressed. Ask ChatGPT, "What's something meaningful my hero could lose that would reshape how they see themselves?" and suddenly, your story's full of weight.

Great stakes make the audience lean in emotionally. If the hero is chasing a missing person, what's the relationship? What history exists between them? If they're protecting a piece of information, what truth does it hold—and what happens if it's lost or exposed? Even something as big as "stop the virus" gets more powerful when the person holding the antidote is the one who let the virus loose in the first place. Ask ChatGPT, "How can I tie the stakes of the mission to the hero's greatest regret?" and the adventure becomes a personal reckoning.

Another level to explore is **moral stakes**. Maybe the hero can win the fight but lose their soul. They could save the day by becoming the thing they swore to destroy. Or they could take an easier path that betrays their values. These moments raise huge tension—because the audience isn't just wondering *if* the hero will succeed, but *how much of themselves they'll lose doing it*. Ask ChatGPT, "What's a decision that could force my hero to choose between their moral code and the mission?" and your story instantly grows teeth.

Sometimes, the stakes are **philosophical**. The hero isn't just protecting people—they're defending an idea. Freedom. Truth. Compassion. Belief in humanity. These stories don't just end in explosions—they end with changed minds. You don't have to be preachy to do this. You just have to show that the outcome of the mission has consequences *beyond the battlefield*. Ask ChatGPT, "How can I build a story where the villain threatens an idea instead of a person?" and now you're writing with intellectual weight behind every chase and punch.

Don't forget **emotional stakes**. A hero might fear death, sure. But what they *really* fear is abandonment. Or letting someone down. Or realizing they're no longer the person they used to be. Maybe their greatest enemy isn't the villain—it's their own guilt. These are the moments where even small victories feel enormous, and failures feel catastrophic. Ask ChatGPT, "What emotional stake could haunt my hero throughout the mission?" and you'll get a thread you can weave into every moment of action.

When stakes go beyond survival, your story gains *reverberation*. Each fight, chase, escape, or loss echoes deeper. The audience doesn't just care what's happening—they care *why* it's happening. They want to see if the hero can not only survive—but grow, heal, change, or redeem something broken. Because it's not just about who walks away—it's about what walking away *costs*.

And here's where it gets really interesting: sometimes, the hero does survive... and still loses. Maybe they save the world but lose the person they love. Maybe they win the battle but realize they've become too much like the enemy. Maybe they keep the secret but now have to live with it. Ask ChatGPT, "Give me three ending ideas where the hero succeeds, but at a heavy emotional price," and you'll find that the impact of your story lasts long after the smoke clears.

When you're writing your story in a day, don't be afraid to chase *big feelings*. That doesn't mean long speeches or melodrama. It means clarity of purpose. Know what your characters want *besides staying alive*. Know what they're willing to die for. Know what they're *not* willing to become. Ask yourself at every turn: "What's at stake in this scene beyond blood and bullets?"

Even your villains can carry this weight. Let them believe in something—even if it's horrifying. Let their loss be real. When both sides believe they're right, the conflict becomes about more than who wins—it becomes about *what kind of world we end up with*. That's the stuff of unforgettable adventure.

So yeah, keep the explosions. Keep the ticking clocks and collapsing caves and rooftop chases.

But also ask: What breaks if the hero fails? What truth dies? What bond is shattered? What part of themselves do they risk never getting back?

Because that's what gives action *consequence*.

And that's what turns adventure into something worth remembering.

Action for Film vs. Action for the Page

Writing action for film and writing action for the page are two very different beasts, even though they might look similar at a glance. On screen, action is all about visual spectacle—movement, timing, editing, sound, and performance. On the page, action lives inside the reader's imagination, and it's powered by language, rhythm, point of view, and pacing. If you're writing an action-adventure story in one day, knowing how to switch gears between writing for the screen and writing for prose is critical. What works brilliantly on camera can fall flat in a novel. And what moves a reader's mind might never translate to a single shot.

So let's break it down.

In film, **action is choreography**. You're directing the scene through visual beats. Every movement, every explosion, every bullet, every fall is visible, often in real-time or even slow motion. You have stunt teams, sound effects, music, and camera work doing the heavy lifting. In a script, that translates to short, sharp sentences. You're giving instructions: "He ducks. Fires. Rolls left. The wall explodes. She screams." Each sentence is a shot, a beat. Pacing is dictated by line breaks. It's clean, fast, and physical. You let the director and the actors do the rest.

In prose, **you are the camera, the sound, the stunts, and the emotion.** You're not just showing the action—you're creating the *experience* of it. That means you can slow time down, zoom in on a trembling hand, let us feel the hero's heartbeat pounding against their ribs, taste the grit in their mouth, or get trapped in the fog of confusion during a brawl. That's where the magic of writing comes in. You don't just describe action—you make the *reader live it.*

For screenwriters, clarity is everything. No flowery language. No deep introspection mid-punch. A screenplay is a blueprint. The action must be filmable. You don't write, "He felt rage boil in his chest." You write, "He glares. His fists clench. He charges." Ask ChatGPT, "Rewrite this paragraph of prose action as a filmable screenplay scene," and it'll snap your language into a director-friendly format.

But for novelists and storytellers writing prose? Go inside. Let the reader *feel* the fear, the desperation, the second-guessing. Let the action pause for one sentence as the hero remembers a training drill. Let the pain sting. Let the sound of the explosion come through the ringing in their ears. You can write: "He tried to breathe, but the dust was everywhere—clogging his throat, burning his lungs. The flash of fire was gone, but his vision still flickered like an old film reel." Ask ChatGPT, "Expand this fight scene into immersive prose with internal thoughts and sensory details," and you'll watch the action come alive on the page.

One of the biggest differences is **how time moves.** In a film, action moves in real-time unless you use slow motion or clever editing. In a novel, you *control time with sentence structure.* Short, clipped sentences speed things up. Long, winding ones slow things down. You can stretch out a three-second fall into a full paragraph of memory, sensation, and emotion. You can compress an entire brawl into two breathless lines. You're not just writing action—you're sculpting time.

Another key difference is **scope of perspective.** On film, we see what the camera shows. In a book, you can be inside the character's head, or float above them, or even follow multiple characters' experiences in the same moment. You can show a fight from the hero's blurry vision—and also reveal the ambush coming from the trees that *they* don't see, but the *reader* does. Ask ChatGPT, "Describe this action scene from a third-person limited point of view to emphasize surprise and confusion," and you'll get a more emotionally textured scene than film can easily convey.

One thing you can't do in film—but *absolutely can* do in prose—is **embed character development inside the action.** Maybe the hero flinches because they once froze in a firefight. Maybe they hesitate to shoot because they see the villain's child in the background. These emotional beats would slow a movie down or require extra shots and scenes—but in a novel, they flow right into the rhythm of the action. Ask ChatGPT, "How can I layer character growth into a high-stakes action scene?" and it'll help you thread those powerful moments into your pacing.

But here's where things come together: if you *combine* cinematic action beats with prose's emotional depth, you create a hybrid style that works for readers who *see* the movie in their heads. You can write lines like: "She dived, rolled, fired—three shots in the dark. One hit. One missed. One hit *him.*" That's film rhythm in novel form. It's punchy, fast, and visual, but still lets the reader into the moment. You can also flip that and write film-ready scripts with just enough emotion or subtext to make it more than a stunt reel.

So when you're writing your action-adventure story in one day, ask yourself: *Am I writing this scene for the screen or for the soul?*

And if you're not sure, ask ChatGPT to show you both versions.

Because once you understand how action lives on screen and breathes on the page, you can make your story hit harder, move faster, and *matter* more.

And that's the kind of action people don't just *watch* or *read*.

That's the kind they *remember.*

Cinematic Writing Tricks with ChatGPT

There's a certain magic that happens when writing feels like a movie playing in your reader's mind. That's cinematic writing. It doesn't mean you're writing a screenplay—it means your words have rhythm, your scenes have movement, your transitions flow like a camera glide, and every image you paint feels like something you could see on the big screen. When you're writing an action-adventure story in one day, cinematic writing isn't just about flair—it's about clarity, energy, and emotional punch. And with ChatGPT at your fingertips, you can use cinematic writing tricks that instantly upgrade your story without grinding to a halt.

Let's start with the basics: **cinematic writing is about what the reader sees and feels**, not just what happens. Instead of telling them, "The explosion was loud," you show them, "The shockwave punched through the alley, shattering windows and flipping a rusted-out car like a toy." The key is to anchor action in vivid imagery. You want your sentences to cut like film edits—clean, sharp, kinetic. You can say to ChatGPT, "Rewrite this paragraph with vivid, cinematic description and sensory detail," and it'll give you a version that feels shot with a Steadicam and scored by Hans Zimmer.

One of the best cinematic tricks is **the wide shot**. That's when you pull the lens back and show us the whole battlefield, temple, jungle, or crumbling city. It's about scale. You can describe the entire environment in one sweeping, high-altitude sentence. Ask ChatGPT, "Describe a cinematic wide shot of a flooded underground cathedral lit by torches," and you'll get a scene opener that drops the reader into the setting with jaw-dropping clarity.

Then you zoom in. You use the **close-up**. Focus on a drop of sweat, a trembling hand, the flicker in someone's eyes before they lie. These small details slow time and ramp up tension. A moment that takes one second in real life can take a whole paragraph if you want it to hit hard. Ask ChatGPT, "Give me a tense, cinematic close-up of a hero realizing their weapon is jammed during a standoff," and you'll get emotional gravity inside physical danger.

Transitions matter, too. Movies use camera movements, jump cuts, and match edits to move smoothly between locations or timelines. You can do the same in your writing. Don't just say, "Later that day." Try, "The sun dipped behind the ridge—and the first rocket lit up the sky." That's a cinematic time cut. Or use action to shift scenes: "The chopper blades cut the silence—then we're back in the jungle, boots hitting mud." Ask ChatGPT, "Help me create a cinematic scene transition that goes from a quiet briefing room to a chaotic battlefield," and you'll get momentum and contrast in one.

Let's talk **sound and silence**. In cinema, sound design is everything. You can hear the ticking of a watch, the slow drag of boots, the sudden hush before a trap springs. On the page, you simulate sound by describing it—and by playing with sentence rhythm. A short, jarring line = a gunshot. A long, slow one = tension rising. Ask ChatGPT, "Write a paragraph that uses sound to build tension in a dark corridor," and you'll hear the creak of the floorboards in your head.

Another cinematic trick? **Parallel action.** That's when two scenes happen at once—cutting back and forth between them for maximum tension. One character is defusing a bomb, the other is holding off enemy forces. You switch between them, sentence by sentence, until the tension breaks. This technique works beautifully on the page. Ask ChatGPT, "Write an example of parallel action between a hacker breaking into a system and a spy infiltrating the same building," and you'll see how storytelling becomes a cross-cutting thrill ride.

Want something cooler? Try **slow motion.** On film, it's used to stretch key moments. On the page, it's done by zooming in on sensory detail and emotion. You describe the moment *before* impact, the flicker of regret in a character's eye, the bead of blood just starting to rise. Ask ChatGPT, "Give me a slow-motion prose moment of a character jumping from a rooftop under gunfire," and you'll get a beat that breathes even as it blazes.

And then there's **montage.** A montage lets you skip the boring parts—training, traveling, setting up traps—while keeping momentum and energy. Use rapid-fire sentences. Punchy visual cues. Let it flow like a sequence of fast cuts. Ask ChatGPT, "Write a cinematic montage of two characters preparing for a dangerous mission," and you'll get a scene that feels like a trailer within your story.

Cinematic writing also means knowing when to **go silent**. A scene without dialogue. A character walking alone through ruins. No noise, just images. This is where your prose becomes pure cinema—visual, atmospheric, loaded with unspoken meaning. Ask ChatGPT, "Write a wordless scene where the hero returns to the battlefield after losing everything," and it'll build silence into something that screams.

And don't forget **symbolic visuals**. In cinema, a shot of a broken watch, a dying flower, or a child's drawing can say more than a line of dialogue. On the page, these same images carry weight. Use them to reinforce your theme or a character's emotional state. Ask ChatGPT, "What are five symbolic visuals I can use to reflect a character's inner turmoil during an action scene?" and you'll add layers without adding exposition.

The secret to cinematic writing is rhythm. Cut when it feels right. Linger when it matters. Write as if you're holding a camera and an audience is breathing down your neck. Make the sentences move the same way the characters do—fluid, intense, relentless.

And whenever you feel stuck or flat, say to ChatGPT:

"Make this read like a movie trailer."

Or:

"Rewrite this action beat like it's a Michael Bay set piece."

Or:

"Add Spielberg-style wonder to this discovery moment."

It's not about copying film—it's about capturing *feeling*. Movement. Awe. Momentum. Visual power on the page.

So go wide. Go tight. Cut fast. Hold slow.

And with ChatGPT right beside you, your action-adventure story will *feel* like a blockbuster...

Even if it was written in just one epic day.

Pacing the Ride: When to Breathe, When to Burn

Pacing is everything in an action-adventure story. It's what makes the difference between a thrilling rollercoaster and a blurry mess of movement. It's not just about speed—it's about rhythm. It's about knowing when to slam the gas pedal to the floor and when to ease off so your characters—and your reader—can take a breath. If you're writing your action-adventure story in one intense day, getting the pacing right means your story won't just be fast—it'll be *gripping*. And that's where ChatGPT becomes your best pacing mechanic.

Think of your story like a pulse. There should be tension, release, tension, release. It's not all one-note. If every scene is a high-octane chase or a firefight, none of them feel intense. They blur. But when you follow a burst of chaos with a beat of quiet reflection, a moment of stillness, or a low hum of suspense, the next action beat hits harder. The contrast is what creates the thrill.

Let's say you've just written a massive action set-piece—a warehouse ambush, maybe, or a high-speed boat chase. You might feel tempted to roll right into another fight or escape. But that's the moment to breathe. Let the characters limp away. Let them catch their breath, clean their wounds, doubt themselves, argue. Maybe they find a clue. Maybe they have a quiet laugh. Maybe they fall apart. These are the scenes that build connection. Ask ChatGPT, "Write a quiet scene between two characters after a near-death escape that deepens their bond without slowing the plot," and you'll have your pacing beat without losing momentum.

Your pacing isn't just about alternating fast and slow—it's about building tension in *layers*. A well-paced story escalates. Each act should feel faster than the last, even if the actual word count per scene doesn't change. You don't throw your biggest explosion in the first ten pages unless you've got something even *wilder* coming later. Ask ChatGPT, "Help me structure three escalating action scenes that each raise the stakes," and you'll get a blueprint that climbs instead of stalls.

You also want to pay attention to **scene length and paragraph flow**. Short, snappy paragraphs create urgency. They're your burn moments. You use them in fights, chases, ticking clocks. Long, winding paragraphs slow the story down. They're your breath moments. You use them when the hero's thinking, feeling, or discovering something. Ask ChatGPT, "Rewrite this chase scene with shorter sentences to increase tension," and you'll instantly feel the speed increase. Or, "Expand this quiet scene with internal thoughts to give the reader a breather," and now the pulse slows to a controlled rest.

Even your dialogue plays into pacing. During action, it should be clipped, reactive, and sharp. Between action, you can let conversations stretch, allow characters to reflect or reveal. You're using dialogue not just to share information, but to control how fast the reader moves. Ask ChatGPT, "Give me a fast-paced exchange between characters arguing mid-mission," and it'll keep the dialogue racing. Then flip the switch: "Write a slower, more vulnerable conversation between the same characters while regrouping," and now your reader exhales without losing interest.

Another trick is to **fake a breather and turn it into a surprise.** You let the reader settle in, thinking the scene is safe, only to flip the switch—ambush, betrayal, collapse. This sudden reversal *feels* faster because it hits from stillness. Ask ChatGPT, "Create a calm scene that ends in an unexpected twist without telegraphing it," and you've got a pacing device that snaps tension like a whip.

The middle of a story is where pacing most often gets messy. You're out of the setup, not yet in the climax, and you risk flatlining. This is where you mix it up. Add a mystery. A reversal. A betrayal. A flashback. A travel montage. A ticking clock. Don't just throw in action for its own sake—make sure it's moving the story forward. Ask ChatGPT, "What kind of twist or reveal can keep the momentum alive at the halfway point?" and you'll get a pacing jolt right when you need it.

And when it comes to **the final act**, you want to ride that burn all the way to the finish. The breath moments become shorter. The scenes come faster. The decisions are irreversible. You want the reader gripping the edge of their seat, flipping pages, feeling that weight of no turning back. Ask ChatGPT, "Help me structure the final sequence so it keeps escalating until the very last moment," and your climax won't just be action—it'll be *inevitable*.

Here's a quick test: read through your story and track how often something changes. Pacing isn't just about speed—it's about *change*. Someone gets new information. Makes a decision. Faces a new obstacle. The more change per page, the faster it feels—even if it's emotionally quiet. Ask ChatGPT, "Analyze this chapter and tell me where the momentum slows," and you'll find your drag points before they sink the ride.

In the end, pacing isn't about cutting breathless scenes together—it's about *controlling the rhythm of tension and release*. A great action-adventure story feels like a heartbeat you can't stop hearing. It pulls you into the rush, slows you down just enough to care, then rockets forward again, faster, sharper, deeper.

And with ChatGPT beside you, helping you tune each scene like a gear in a well-oiled engine, you're not just writing fast.

You're writing with *precision*.

Because the best stories don't sprint from start to finish.

They *breathe*.

Then they *burn*.

And then they *explode*.

Dialogue during Chaos: Talking in Explosions

One of the wildest balancing acts in action-adventure writing is getting dialogue to work during the loudest, messiest, most chaotic scenes in your story. You've got bullets flying, debris raining from the ceiling, alarms blaring, and two characters still find time to argue about directions, make snarky comments, confess feelings, or bark critical information. Done well, this kind of dialogue doesn't just add flavor—it grounds the reader, sharpens character dynamics, and makes the action feel personal. Done wrong, it's confusing or cheesy. When you're writing a full action-adventure story in a single day, learning to write dialogue in the heat of chaos can turn your big scenes from basic to unforgettable.

The trick is to remember that **dialogue during chaos isn't about long speeches—it's about *urgency* and *personality*.** People don't explain things during a car crash. They shout, grunt, curse, snap orders. Think of it like writing text that *feels like shouting over the noise*—short, sharp, loaded with tension or sarcasm or panic. Ask ChatGPT, "Write five short lines of dialogue a hero might yell while hanging from a burning rope bridge," and you'll get the rhythm that fits the scene.

One of the easiest and most cinematic uses of dialogue in chaos is **conflict under pressure**. Two characters who can't stand each other are forced to work together. The bomb is ticking, the floor is crumbling, and they're still bickering. These exchanges don't just break tension with humor—they *highlight stakes*. If these two stop arguing, one of them might die. Ask ChatGPT, "Write an action scene with two characters arguing while fighting off enemies," and you'll get both tension and personality without stopping the flow.

Now, there's another kind of dialogue you can use mid-chaos: **urgent, clipped info-drops.** A character shouts out directions, warns of incoming danger, or passes on a key piece of information *on the move*. "Left! LEFT!" "She's got the detonator!" "Cover me—I'm going in!" These lines are part of the action, not separate from it. They let the reader *track* what's happening in fast, noisy scenes. Ask ChatGPT, "Give me examples of urgent action dialogue used during a rescue sequence under fire," and you'll have your tactical language ready.

Another fun technique is **dark humor or sarcasm** in life-or-death moments. This works great in buddy-cop style dynamics or when your hero is the kind who keeps it cool under pressure by being funny. "Tell me again why we *aren't* taking the elevator?" "This was *your* plan!" "At least the explosion wasn't *boring*." Humor doesn't lower the stakes—it gives the chaos texture. It also reminds us that your characters are *thinking, reacting human beings*, not just action dolls. Ask ChatGPT, "Write a sequence where two characters exchange sarcastic banter while escaping through a collapsing tunnel," and watch the chemistry come to life.

When writing dialogue during chaos, **timing matters**. You want to place each line where the tension spikes or pivots. Dialogue can *interrupt* a moment ("You hear that?" right before an explosion), *react* to it ("Oh, hell—here we go again!"), or *redirect* it ("No, not that wire!"). Dialogue works like a steering wheel for the reader—it helps them follow the scene even when everything's exploding around them. Ask ChatGPT, "Help me pace a scene where dialogue guides a fast-paced rooftop chase," and you'll keep the action readable and exciting.

Let's not forget the **emotional punch** that can come through during intense moments. A character might scream a confession as the room collapses. Or promise to come back just before jumping into danger. These are risky but powerful beats if you keep them short and raw. You don't need speeches. You just need a few words that hit with the force of the moment. Ask ChatGPT, "Write a high-emotion one-liner shouted during an explosion that reveals a hidden truth," and you'll add heart to the spectacle.

If your action is especially chaotic, **use silence strategically**. Someone says something—and it's drowned out by gunfire. A name is screamed—but unheard. These near-misses can be as dramatic as the lines themselves. You create *emotional static*. Ask ChatGPT, "Give me examples of partially-heard or interrupted dialogue in an action scene," and you'll have moments that feel real and cinematic.

Now, on a technical level: **don't over-tag**. In chaos, the rhythm is fast. You don't need "he shouted," "she screamed," "they hollered" after every line. Often, you can strip it down. Let the context and punctuation do the work. Dialogue lines stand out better when the surrounding action is tight and clear. But if you want help polishing, just paste the dialogue into ChatGPT and say, "Clean this action scene dialogue to read fast and natural under pressure," and it'll optimize the pacing for you.

Another powerful move is using **dialogue to raise the stakes in real time.** "The whole building's wired!" "We've got thirty seconds!" "They're already inside!" These aren't just updates—they're gut punches. They shift the entire scene. Ask ChatGPT, "Write an action scene where a single line of dialogue changes the mission entirely," and you'll see how dialogue can become the *engine* of the chaos.

When you combine character dynamics, urgency, and rhythm, dialogue in action becomes more than just words—it becomes *fuel*. The right line, at the right moment, makes the scene unforgettable. It humanizes the spectacle. It builds pressure. It breaks tension. It reveals character under fire.

So next time you drop your characters into the middle of mayhem—

Let them speak.

Let them shout.

Let them joke, snap, confess, argue, warn, or whisper just before the big blast.

And if you're not sure what they'd say?

Just ask ChatGPT:

"What would this character yell if everything was going wrong and they only had one shot to make it right?"

Because sometimes, the best line in the story...

Is screamed over the roar of everything falling apart.

Traps, Clues, and Ancient Puzzles

If you want to give your action-adventure story that classic, pulse-racing, treasure-hunting vibe, there's no better combo than traps, clues, and ancient puzzles. This is the holy trinity of mystery and movement—where brains meet brawn, where danger hides in dust-covered silence, and where solving the riddle wrong could mean triggering a centuries-old death machine. Whether you're writing about a forgotten temple in the jungle or a lost underground city beneath a modern metropolis, these elements make the adventure feel alive. And when you're writing your story in one day, ChatGPT can help you build them fast, deep, and deadly.

Let's start with traps. They're not just about spikes and swinging axes—though there's nothing wrong with a good swinging axe. Great traps are part of the setting's logic. They protect something. They punish intruders. They test worthiness. They're ancient warnings that the next step could be your last. You want to create traps that *fit* the world—mechanisms that are just believable enough to make readers think, "Yeah, someone could've built that... maybe."

Ask ChatGPT, "Give me five creative ancient traps for a tomb that hasn't been opened in 1,000 years," and you'll get more than pressure plates and dart holes. You might get rooms that fill with sand, mirrors that redirect light to ignite oil, doors that lock from the outside, or puzzles that must be solved under time pressure—or else.

Now, what about clues? Clues are the breadcrumbs your characters follow, but they're not just there for the plot—they're tools to *engage the reader*. A well-placed clue invites your audience to lean in, to wonder, to guess. Maybe it's a symbol carved into stone, a phrase that appears in multiple languages, or a statue that doesn't match the others. The best clues aren't just dropped—they're *hidden in plain sight*.

Ask ChatGPT, "Give me subtle clues hidden in a Roman-era artifact that point to a forgotten battle site," and you'll start weaving mystery into your set pieces. The idea is to make every discovery feel earned. You want the reader and the character to gasp at the same time.

Ancient puzzles are the brainy cousin to traps—they don't kill you outright, but they will if you get them wrong. Riddles, shifting stones, light patterns, coded languages, mazes, musical notes, or even memory-based sequences. The fun part of these puzzles isn't just solving them—it's what happens *if they're not* solved. Or what happens *after* they are. A door opens... but the floor starts collapsing. A statue moves... and releases something best left buried.

Ask ChatGPT, "Design an ancient puzzle that requires characters to use elements from earlier in the story," and you'll build something that doesn't just challenge the characters—it *rewards the reader* for paying attention. That's when the whole story starts feeling like one big, interconnected system. Nothing is random. Everything means something.

Another great trick is the **false puzzle**—something that looks like a puzzle, but is really a distraction, a trap, or a test of character. The idea isn't to outsmart the puzzle, but to *resist* the urge to solve it. Maybe the treasure's in plain sight, and the real trap is the mechanism that activates when someone moves the decoy. Ask ChatGPT, "Write a fake puzzle scene that tests a character's greed," and you'll suddenly have moral tension laced into your mystery.

Don't forget to layer your clues across locations. Maybe there's a map—but it's incomplete. Maybe there's a poem—but the last verse is missing. Each location your characters visit gives them a piece of the full answer, but they won't understand the meaning until the pieces are combined. You can build your whole story around this: "Find the four objects, decode the message, reach the hidden site." Ask ChatGPT, "Create a four-part ancient riddle that guides characters across continents," and now your plot is structured like a scavenger hunt for the bold and desperate.

Also, make the puzzles **personal**. Let them reflect the fears or flaws of your characters. Maybe the puzzle is easy for someone brave but impossible for someone who panics. Maybe it requires someone to admit a secret. Maybe it echoes a decision the character made in the past—forcing them to relive it. Ask ChatGPT, "Design a puzzle that forces a character to confront their past mistake in order to solve it," and your plot just got emotional real fast.

Let's not forget the villain. Traps, clues, and puzzles aren't just for heroes. The antagonist might be solving them too—or *leaving behind* false ones to delay or sabotage the hero. Maybe the villain solved the puzzle long ago, stole the treasure, and rigged the clues to lead competitors into disaster. You can turn the whole adventure into a race, with the hero slowly realizing they're walking in the footsteps of someone far more ruthless. Ask ChatGPT, "Write a scene where the hero realizes the clues have been tampered with by the villain," and now your suspense level just hit red.

And remember: not every puzzle has to be ancient. Sometimes, modern clues overlay the old ones. A hacker deciphers symbols. A drone reveals a map. A digital key leads to an analog tomb. The blend of old and new gives your story range and freshness. Ask ChatGPT, "Combine ancient temple puzzles with modern technology used by the characters," and you'll create scenes that feel classic and current at the same time.

In the end, traps, clues, and puzzles turn your story into an experience. They force your characters to think. They turn the environment into an active player. They make every step forward feel dangerous, earned, and exhilarating.

And with ChatGPT helping you build the bones of those deadly puzzles, twisted clues, and ingenious traps, you're not just writing another chase.

You're writing a story that *tests* your characters—and rewards your reader.

So go ahead.

Spring the trap.

Hide the key.

Whisper the answer in a forgotten tongue.

And let the game begin.

Working from a Beat Sheet Built by ChatGPT

If you want to write an action-adventure story in one day without losing your grip on structure, pacing, or character arcs, a beat sheet is your secret weapon. A beat sheet is like a skeleton for your story—it lays out the major turning points, emotional moments, and action beats that will keep everything flowing from page one to the final scene. The beauty of it? With ChatGPT, you don't have to build one alone. In fact, you can have a complete, customized beat sheet ready in minutes, tailored to your characters, your tone, your genre twists, and even your personal writing style. That kind of power is a game-changer when you've got one day to make magic happen.

A traditional beat sheet might feel a little rigid or overly academic. But when you use ChatGPT to create one, it becomes fluid and intuitive. It becomes your *map* through the jungle. You're not wandering around hoping for inspiration—you're on a mission, and each beat is a stepping stone to the next big moment.

Let's say you've got a general idea: a rogue archaeologist must stop a corrupt billionaire from unearthing an ancient weapon buried in the Himalayas. That's enough to get started. Now you just prompt ChatGPT with something like, "Create a 15-beat outline for an action-adventure story where a rogue archaeologist must stop a corrupt billionaire from unearthing an ancient weapon." And just like that, the framework arrives—opening scene, inciting incident, midpoint twist, climax, all there.

Here's where it gets fun. You can keep refining the beats on the fly. Want more emotional weight? Ask, "Add internal conflict beats where the protagonist struggles with guilt from a past failure." Want a sidekick? Ask, "Weave a reluctant partner character into the beat sheet who later sacrifices themselves." Want it to feel like *Indiana Jones meets John Wick*? Just say so. ChatGPT adapts instantly. It's like having a story architect who never gets tired, never runs out of ideas, and never says, "Let me get back to you."

What makes working from a beat sheet so powerful is that it gives you permission to **focus on writing scenes, not solving structure**. You already know what happens next. You're not guessing what the midpoint should be. You're not stuck trying to figure out how the chase scene fits into the larger arc. The beats give you purpose. And when you pair them with the right prompts, you can ask ChatGPT to flesh out any moment instantly.

Let's break that down. Say you're at Beat 6: "Hero breaks into the villain's private collection and finds a stolen artifact." You can now ask ChatGPT, "Write a cinematic action scene where the hero sneaks into the villain's private collection, is almost caught, and discovers an ancient artifact that reveals a hidden location." You get the full sensory scene. Then refine it: "Make the dialogue snappy and sarcastic, and add a moment of awe when they uncover the artifact." And boom—your draft isn't just functional, it's dynamic.

Using a beat sheet also helps manage **pacing**, because you can see where the action rises and falls. You'll know if you're spending too long on setup or if the final act needs more punch. ChatGPT can even audit your beat sheet. Ask, "Does this story structure escalate tension properly?" or "Where should I add a twist to make Act Two stronger?" and you'll get story-savvy feedback in real time.

Let's say you've got a standard 3-act structure:

1. **Act One** (Setup and inciting incident)
2. **Act Two** (Rising tension, midpoint reversal, and dark moment)
3. **Act Three** (Climax and resolution)

With ChatGPT, you can go even deeper. Ask for genre-specific beats:

"Add genre-specific beats for a globe-trotting treasure hunt action story."

"Give me a variation where the hero fails at the climax but wins emotionally."

"Break this into chapter-sized beats for a 20-chapter book."

You don't have to memorize Save the Cat or read three screenwriting guides—you've got a responsive co-writer who can customize structure on demand.

You can even collaborate with ChatGPT live as you write. At Beat 8 you might pause and think, "I need a unique trap room puzzle here." Ask, "What kind of ancient puzzle could block the entrance to a lost mountain vault, with deadly consequences if solved wrong?" And the beat explodes into a fully-formed scene, complete with visual cues, clues, and character reactions.

If your story starts veering off course, the beat sheet pulls you back in. Or you can adjust the beats to follow the new direction. You're not locked in—you're *equipped*. Ask, "Rewrite the final three beats with a twist where the hero is betrayed by their partner," and suddenly the ending reshapes itself into something even more powerful.

And remember, you don't have to follow every beat to the letter. The sheet is your guide, not your prison. You can merge beats, flip their order, cut what doesn't serve the emotional arc, or combine two beats into one high-stakes sequence. Ask ChatGPT, "Which of these beats could be combined to make the pacing tighter?" and it'll give you a streamlined path without breaking the story.

The real magic is that when you build your story on a beat sheet made with ChatGPT, you free your mind to focus on what matters most: writing with momentum. You stop wondering where you're going and start enjoying the ride.

Because in the end, a good action-adventure story is about forward motion.

A beat sheet gives that motion *direction*.

And ChatGPT gives that direction *fuel*.

So before you write your next line, just ask yourself:

What's the next beat?

And if you don't know—

ChatGPT always does.

Flashbacks, Time Jumps, and Story Layers

In the world of action-adventure storytelling, time is a tool—and when you know how to bend it, you can do more than just tell a story. You can shape it. Flashbacks, time jumps, and layered storytelling give your narrative depth, suspense, and emotional power. They let you reveal things when they matter most, not when they happened. They give your characters history. They let the past interrupt the present. And when used right, they make the difference between a simple sequence of events and a gripping, cinematic experience that feels like it matters.

And yes, even if you're writing your action-adventure story in just one day, time tricks like these can be built quickly and cleverly—with ChatGPT doing the heavy lifting right alongside you.

Let's start with flashbacks. These are one of the most common and powerful ways to give a character—or a location, or an artifact—meaning. Maybe the hero's climbing the same cliff where they once failed to save someone. Maybe they hear a phrase the villain says and it sparks a memory from childhood. Flashbacks don't just tell us what happened—they tell us *why* it matters now. They make action personal.

A great flashback doesn't interrupt the momentum—it *sharpens it.* The best ones are triggered by something in the present: a place, a sound, an object, a smell, a line of dialogue. And they're short. Tight. Focused. They don't explain everything. They offer just enough to change how the character—and the reader—sees what's happening in the now.

Ask ChatGPT, "Write a short flashback scene that reveals why the hero is terrified of water, right as they're about to jump into a river," and you'll get a piece that's emotionally charged and plot-relevant in the same breath.

Then there are time jumps. You can leap forward or backward in time to create mystery, structure your story non-linearly, or keep your pacing fresh. Sometimes, you don't want to show how they got from the jungle to the city—you just want to cut to the rooftop chase that happens after. Or maybe you start your story in the middle of the final battle, and then jump back to how it all began. That's a classic move: begin at the climax, make us care, then rewind and show us how everything fell into place—or fell apart.

This works especially well when the story hinges on a twist, a betrayal, or a long-buried truth. Time jumps let you play with audience expectations. You can reveal something in Act Three that reframes what we thought we knew about Act One. Ask ChatGPT, "How can I open my story with a final scene, then jump back in time and keep the structure engaging?" and you'll get a map of narrative tension to follow.

Story layering is the big picture version of all this. It's not just about jumping in time—it's about *weaving timelines and character threads together* so they echo, reflect, and intensify one another. The past informs the present. The present affects how we see the past. And the future hangs in the balance between the two. When done right, layered storytelling makes every moment feel like a puzzle piece—and the reader doesn't get the full image until the last scene clicks into place.

One great way to do this is to run two timelines side by side. A young version of the hero going through a similar ordeal as their current self. Or the antagonist's rise happening in parallel with the hero's fall. Each scene in one thread echoes or contrasts with the other. Ask ChatGPT, "Build two interwoven timelines—one past and one present—for a story about a treasure hunter retracing their mentor's last expedition," and you'll get a beautifully layered setup that writes itself.

Another smart move is to use flashbacks to *hide answers*. Let the characters misremember. Let them block out key details. Then reveal the truth later. Maybe the hero believes they were betrayed—but the flashback twists later to show the betrayal was a sacrifice. Maybe the villain's cruelty is rooted in something misunderstood. These reversals don't just change the plot—they *charge* it with emotional weight. Ask ChatGPT, "Write a flashback that looks heroic at first, but later is revealed to be a lie," and now your narrative has layers the audience will peel back like clues in a vault.

Layering also works with locations. A place might appear in the story early as just a cool setting—but later it returns, this time filled with new meaning. A ruined village that was once the hero's childhood home. A mountaintop that holds both victory and tragedy. Ask ChatGPT, "Help me build a location with layered meaning tied to both the hero's past and the final battle," and you'll get a setting that grows in importance every time it appears.

One of the biggest strengths of using flashbacks and layered storytelling is that you don't need to explain everything at once. You can trust the reader to follow. You can *build intrigue*. You can drop a name without context, then drop the memory ten chapters later. You can flash back to the *wrong moment on purpose*—and then later, show what *really* happened. This lets you shape the reader's emotional journey, not just the plotline. Ask ChatGPT, "Create a sequence of flashbacks that slowly reveal a buried secret without giving it away too early," and you'll end up with breadcrumbs instead of info dumps.

And when it comes to one-day writing marathons, this kind of structure lets you keep energy up by jumping around in time. If you're getting bored with the middle act, skip to the dramatic flashback or the flash-forward epilogue and build backwards. Structure doesn't have to be linear—it just has to be *clear*. You can always connect the beats later. And if you're stuck, just tell ChatGPT: "Organize my flashbacks and time jumps into a clear order that builds tension," and your tangled wires turn into a smooth circuit.

In the end, flashbacks, time jumps, and story layers aren't just fancy narrative tricks. They're how you *reveal character*, *build mystery*, and *create emotional payoffs*. They're how you show what happened, what mattered, and why it still echoes through every action, every choice, every explosion.

Because the past doesn't just haunt your hero—it *drives* them.

And time, when it's broken and stitched back together the right way, can turn even the fastest-paced story into something unforgettable.

Making the Climax Satisfy After All That Build-Up

You've spent the whole story building toward this moment. The traps have been triggered, the secrets unearthed, the allies tested, the villains revealed, and the stakes raised again and again until it all reaches a boiling point. The climax. It's where everything converges—action, emotion, revelation, and resolve. And in an action-adventure story, the climax isn't just about explosions or final punches. It's about payoffs. It's about *satisfaction*. When the story's heart finally beats its loudest. When the audience gets everything they've been waiting for—whether it's a long-delayed showdown, a hidden truth, or a sacrifice that changes everything.

When you're writing your action-adventure in one day, the climax can be the trickiest part to get right. You're tired. You've already covered so much ground. You're racing to the finish line. But here's the truth: *the climax defines the story*. A weak one can undo all the good will you've built. A strong one can make everything that came before it feel legendary.

Let's start here—**the climax must answer the central question of the story**. What was the hero trying to do all along? What were they afraid of? What did they need to overcome? The climax is not just the biggest explosion or the most impressive fight—it's the moment that *resolves the emotional arc*. Ask ChatGPT, "What's the emotional resolution my hero needs to face in the climax based on this arc?" and you'll find the missing piece that makes it personal, not just physical.

Your climax needs to be **earned**. You can't drop a new character or twist out of nowhere and expect it to feel right. Everything in the final sequence must feel like it grew naturally from the story that came before. That artifact in Chapter 2? It has to matter now. That scar mentioned in passing? Now we understand where it came from. The quiet moment of doubt at the midpoint? It pays off when the hero refuses to run. Ask ChatGPT, "List the threads I've introduced in this story and how they could pay off in the climax," and you'll have a checklist to make your ending feel like the final chord of a symphony.

Let's talk action. The climax doesn't have to be the longest action sequence, but it should be the most intense, most personal, most revealing. It's not about the number of punches thrown—it's about what's *at stake in every punch*. Maybe the villain and hero have history. Maybe the hero has to choose between revenge and justice. Maybe they're physically overmatched but emotionally prepared. Ask ChatGPT, "Write a final confrontation that combines physical stakes with emotional closure," and the scene practically writes itself.

Also, remember the **setting of the climax matters**. This is your moment to go big, weird, dramatic, symbolic—whatever fits the tone. Maybe they're battling on a crumbling skybridge over lava. Maybe they're racing to stop a countdown in an ancient machine chamber. Maybe they're underwater, or at the top of a storm-wracked mountain. Wherever it is, make it *mean* something. It should reflect the theme or echo something from earlier. Ask ChatGPT, "Suggest a setting for the climax that symbolically reflects the hero's journey," and you'll add depth without slowing down the pace.

The climax is also a chance to **twist the knife** one last time. Not every final confrontation should be predictable. Maybe the villain was right. Maybe the ally betrays them. Maybe the hero's victory requires a loss they didn't expect. But be careful—this isn't the time to get clever just for shock value. Any twist here has to *feel* right. Ask ChatGPT, "Give me a twist in the climax that feels surprising but inevitable," and you'll have a moment your readers didn't see coming—but will realize they should have.

And don't forget to involve **your supporting cast**. If you've been building allies and relationships, let those characters play a role in the resolution. Maybe they hold off the enemy forces so the hero can go after the villain. Maybe they sacrifice themselves. Maybe the final puzzle requires something only they understand. A climax that *uses everyone* feels epic. Ask ChatGPT, "How can my side characters meaningfully contribute to the climax without overshadowing the protagonist?" and you'll make your cast feel like more than background noise.

Here's something else: **keep the stakes crystal clear**. The reader should know *exactly* what will happen if the hero fails—and it has to be worse than death. It could be the destruction of a city. The fall of an idea. The death of hope. A loved one lost. Or the hero becoming the thing they hate. Ask ChatGPT, "What's a high-stakes consequence that's worse than death for the climax of my action-adventure story?" and you'll sharpen your ending like a blade.

Finally, once the dust settles, you need a **moment of stillness**. A breath. A look. A last line that lingers. Let the character absorb what just happened. Let the reader feel the echo. Did they win? Did they lose something along the way? What changed? The ending doesn't have to be happy—but it does need to feel like an *end*. Ask ChatGPT, "Write a closing moment that gives emotional closure after a climactic battle," and you'll walk away from the story with resonance, not just relief.

In the end, a great climax isn't about going bigger. It's about going *deeper*. It's where plot becomes purpose. Where movement becomes meaning. Where the journey ends—not with just a bang, but with a *truth*.

So give the readers what they didn't even know they were waiting for.

Make them feel the final impact.

And if you ever wonder what it needs?

Just ask ChatGPT:

"How do I make this climax unforgettable?"

And watch it all come together.

The Final Escape or Showdown

Every action-adventure story, no matter how wild or twisty or layered, eventually barrels toward a final moment where there's no more running, no more hiding, and no more backup. Whether it's a daring escape from a collapsing fortress, a brutal one-on-one battle with the villain, or a high-stakes choice that changes everything, the final escape or showdown is the part your readers came for—and the part they'll remember if you do it right. It's the payoff. The cinematic drop-the-mic moment. The last big swing before the story exhales.

When you're writing a full story in one day, this scene is your grand finale, and it deserves to land with impact. Not just because it's the loudest or most explosive part—but because *everything has led to it*. Every trap, twist, and tense stare now funnels into a single confrontation or narrow window of escape. The trick is making sure the scene feels earned, emotionally loaded, and still full of surprise—even if we all knew this moment was coming.

There are two paths the story can take here: **the escape**, or **the showdown**—and sometimes, both. Let's talk escape first.

A final escape isn't just running away. It's surviving the impossible. It's the temple collapsing behind the hero while they sprint across a crumbling bridge. It's the sub filling with water, the plane nosediving, the villain's compound set to blow with ten seconds left on the clock. But more than that, a good escape scene *echoes the theme of the story*. The hero isn't just escaping a place—they're escaping who they used to be. They're breaking free from guilt, from fear, from the past. Ask ChatGPT, "Describe a symbolic final escape from an underwater tomb that parallels the hero's emotional rebirth," and suddenly your action moment is doing double duty.

Final escapes are also the perfect time for callbacks. That seemingly random line from early in the story? Let the hero use it now. That piece of gear they've been carrying? It matters here. That joke that used to be funny? It turns serious. Ask ChatGPT, "Write a final escape scene that pays off three earlier story moments," and you'll get a rush of story glue that ties the whole narrative together in motion.

Now, the final **showdown** is a different kind of beast. This is where it gets personal. Maybe the villain is a twisted reflection of the hero. Maybe the battle isn't just physical—it's ideological. Maybe it's less about who wins and more about *what the hero chooses*. Do they spare the villain? Do they sacrifice themselves? Do they fight dirty or rise above?

You want this scene to be *clear*, *tight*, and *earned*. This isn't the time for a sudden skill upgrade or a convenient last-minute save. The showdown needs to show *who your hero is now*, in contrast to who they were at the start. Ask ChatGPT, "Write a final confrontation that tests the hero's values more than their strength," and you'll get a scene where the fight reveals character.

The setting matters here, too. A great showdown is framed by a powerful location. The rooftop of a burning palace. The edge of a cliff. A quiet, sacred place where violence is forbidden. These spaces aren't just backdrops—they're part of the drama. Ask ChatGPT, "Create a dramatic setting for a final showdown that visually reflects the story's emotional conflict," and the scene practically writes itself.

Sometimes the showdown *isn't* a fight—it's a standoff. A negotiation. A race against time. A sacrifice. The best climaxes aren't predictable—they turn. Maybe the villain has a surprise. Maybe the hero does. Maybe they both lose. Ask ChatGPT, "Give me three unique final confrontation ideas that don't involve a traditional fight," and you'll start breaking out of the usual mold.

Want to do both? Escape and showdown in one? Perfect. Start with the battle, end with the getaway. Or vice versa. Let the hero fight their way out, only to realize they have to make a moral choice on the other side. Let the villain die—but in a way that leaves the hero changed, not triumphant. Ask ChatGPT, "Write a combined final showdown and escape scene where the villain's defeat causes the location to self-destruct," and you've got a high-stakes sequence that delivers the full experience.

Emotion is key. Let the characters *feel* the moment. Let their choices show what they've learned. Even if your hero walks away with cuts and scars and nothing left in their backpack, the reader should *feel* like something meaningful was won.

And don't forget your closing beat. After the escape or the final blow is dealt, give the audience one final breath. The smoke clears. The dust settles. The hero looks back—or maybe doesn't. Maybe they walk away into the unknown, changed forever. Ask ChatGPT, "Write a quiet closing moment after a chaotic final escape," and you'll land the story with grace, not just noise.

So when you reach this part of your one-day writing sprint, don't rush it. Take a deep breath. Picture the movie in your head. Hear the music swell. Feel the gravity of every word, every choice, every movement.

Because whether your hero wins, loses, or limps away...

This is the part they'll carry with them.

And this is the part your reader will remember.

Let them escape.

Let them fight.

But most of all—

Let it *mean something.*

Writing a Pilot Episode for an Action Series

Writing a pilot episode for an action series is a whole different beast from writing a standalone action-adventure story. It's not just about thrilling moments or big fights—it's about introducing a *world* that promises more thrills, more fights, and more depth to come. A great pilot doesn't just hook the viewer or reader—it *locks them in* and makes them say, "I need to know what happens next." So when you sit down to write your action series pilot, especially if you're doing it in a single day with ChatGPT at your side, you're not just writing a first episode—you're designing a launchpad for something much bigger.

The first thing to understand is that **a pilot is a promise**. You're not resolving everything in one episode. You're planting the seeds. You're showing what kind of action this series will deliver, who the key players are, and what kinds of emotional and narrative arcs will unfold over time. It's like the first chapter of a novel combined with the best scenes from a summer blockbuster—tight, fast, but rich with future potential.

Start with a **central hook**. What's the concept that sets this show apart from the dozens of other action series out there? Is it the setting? The mission? The main character's unique skillset or backstory? The tone? Ask ChatGPT, "Help me come up with a high-concept premise for an action series involving a rogue agent and a hidden war," and you'll get an idea that's tailor-made to kick off an epic run.

Once you've got the concept, the next thing is **the hero**. You need to introduce them in a way that tells us exactly what kind of person they are. Not with dialogue or exposition, but with action. Maybe we meet them on a job gone wrong. Maybe they're in hiding. Maybe they're already fighting for something, even if they don't understand why yet. The key is to show them doing something that defines them. Ask ChatGPT, "Write an opening scene that introduces a morally grey hero in the middle of a botched black-ops mission," and you'll start the pilot off with impact.

A good pilot also needs to build out **the world quickly**. You don't need to dump all the details, but we need to know the rules. Is this a near-future tech world? Is there a secret war? Are there factions or shadow governments? Keep it lean, but strong. Show it through visuals, brief dialogue, or background details. Ask ChatGPT, "Give me a concise way to reveal a high-tech dystopian world through dialogue and action in a pilot episode," and the exposition will unfold invisibly while the plot keeps moving.

You also want to establish **the villain or threat**, even if it's in shadows. Maybe the antagonist isn't revealed fully yet, but the *effect* of their actions should be felt. A murdered ally. A stolen device. A town wiped off the map. The threat should hang over everything, making the world feel unstable, dangerous, and urgent. Ask ChatGPT, "Write a teaser scene for a pilot where an unknown enemy strikes before anyone sees them," and you'll create intrigue that pulls viewers forward.

One of the best moves in an action series pilot is to show **one complete mission or event**—something that stands on its own but cracks open the door to the bigger arc. Maybe your hero's hired to retrieve something, but they find something else. Maybe they rescue someone who knows too much. Maybe they're framed, and what starts as a simple job turns into a war against their own agency. The pilot should feel like a story in its own right, *but* with loose threads dangling by the end.

Structure it like this: open big. Hit a short breather. Set up the team or key relationships. Introduce the core conflict. Escalate. Twist. And end with a hook. That hook is what keeps the audience coming back. Ask ChatGPT, "Build me a pilot outline with a strong cold open, rising action, and a cliffhanger ending that sets up the rest of the series," and you'll get a clean roadmap to fill in scene by scene.

Don't forget **supporting characters**. If this is a series, you'll need characters with long-term arcs. A loyal friend with a secret agenda. A rival-turned-reluctant ally. A handler who knows more than they admit. In the pilot, you want to give each of them a strong, clear entrance—something memorable. Ask ChatGPT, "Write an introduction scene for a tough-but-funny hacker sidekick who's pulled back into action," and suddenly your team has depth and flavor.

Dialogue in a pilot should do double duty. It should sound cool and clean—but also reveal character, stakes, or backstory through implication. Think subtext. Think tension. Think banter that carries weight. Ask ChatGPT, "Write a short dialogue exchange that introduces unresolved history between the hero and their ex-partner while they disarm a bomb," and you'll have plot and emotion wrapped in a single beat.

Now—pacing. A great pilot moves fast, but not too fast. Give room to breathe between action scenes. A flashback. A moment of doubt. A close call. That rhythm makes the big scenes land harder. Use ChatGPT to balance it out. "Add a quiet character beat after this action sequence that hints at the hero's trauma," and your script or story suddenly breathes and deepens.

Finally, end on something that *demands the next episode*. Maybe it's a twist. A betrayal. A mysterious symbol. A voice on the other end of a secure line. Something that reframes what we thought we knew. Something that promises bigger battles, harder choices, deeper stakes.

And if you're tired or uncertain at this stage, ask ChatGPT:

"What's the best cliffhanger to end a pilot episode about a rogue team uncovering a global conspiracy?"

It'll give you endings that practically beg for a season.

Because at the end of the day, writing a pilot isn't just about kicking off a story—it's about launching a *series*. And when your audience gets to that last page or that final moment and thinks, *I'm in,* you've done your job.

And if you ever forget what that job is?

Just remember:

Start strong.

Build fast.

End sharp.

And always leave them wanting more.

Turning Your Idea into a Series Bible

So you've written your explosive pilot episode, your characters are popping off the page, and you've got a solid handle on your world, your tone, your action, and the deeper emotional journey beneath all the car chases and ancient puzzles. Now it's time to take the next big step in turning your action-adventure story into a full-on series. That step is building your **series bible**—the behind-the-scenes document that organizes your creative chaos and tells everyone from producers to collaborators exactly what your show is, where it's going, and why it's worth making.

Think of the series bible as your master blueprint. It's not just for pitching (though that's one of its biggest uses)—it's for *you*, the writer. It's how you keep track of the moving pieces. It's the big-picture vision that keeps you from wandering off course once you're deep into episode six and wondering what the villain's long game actually is. And with ChatGPT by your side, you can build the entire thing quickly, clearly, and creatively, even if you're building your action-adventure universe in just a day.

Let's break it down.

The first section of your series bible is **The Series Overview**. This is your show in a nutshell—just a few sharp paragraphs that explain the premise, tone, and hook. What's the concept? What makes this series unique? What kind of action can viewers expect, and what emotional journey lies beneath all the stunts? Think of it as the "elevator pitch meets back-cover blurb." Ask ChatGPT, "Write a series overview for an action-adventure show about an ex-military treasure hunter racing a secret society across the globe," and you've already got your intro done.

Next is **The World**. This is where you explain the setting or settings of your story. Is it globe-trotting like *Indiana Jones* or mostly grounded in one gritty city like *The Punisher*? Is the world modern, historical, futuristic, or a mix? Are there secret factions, hidden technologies, mythological artifacts, or ancient ruins with deadly secrets? This section sets the rules of reality—or how you bend them. Ask ChatGPT, "Describe the world of a high-tech, near-future action series with rogue agents and corporate warlords," and you've got the foundation of your visual and narrative style.

Then you move on to **Characters**. Start with your hero. Who are they, what drives them, what haunts them, and what do they want? Then move to your core supporting cast—your sidekick, your tech expert, your inside mole, your rival, your main antagonist. For each, you want a short bio that includes personality, skillset, personal stakes, and how they evolve over the season. Ask ChatGPT, "Create character bios for a rogue hero, a loyal hacker, and a mysterious antagonist for an action-adventure series," and you'll have instant entries for your bible.

You'll also want to include **Character Arcs**. This goes deeper into how each major character changes over time. Where do they start, what do they face, and where are they headed emotionally, psychologically, and relationally by the end of the season? A character who starts as reckless may learn restraint. A cold, tactical leader may rediscover their heart. Ask ChatGPT, "Map out a character arc for a hero who must overcome their addiction to vengeance," and now your action isn't just loud—it's *meaningful*.

Now comes **The Season Arc**. This is your roadmap of how the story unfolds across episodes. What's the overarching plot or mission? What major events or twists happen along the way? You don't need to spell out every single episode yet—just the tentpole moments. The midpoint twist. The episode where everything falls apart. The big reveal. The climactic confrontation. Ask ChatGPT, "Create a 10-episode season arc for an action series involving a global conspiracy and ancient codes," and you'll have your beats ready to expand.

After that, include **Episode Synopses**. These are 1-2 paragraph breakdowns of each planned episode. If you're writing fast, just focus on the first season. Each summary should show how that episode advances the plot, reveals character, or delivers a must-see action set piece. Ask ChatGPT, "Generate episode summaries for a 6-part action series set in the ruins of a cursed civilization," and boom—you've got your outline in digestible form.

It also helps to have a section on **Themes and Tone**. What is your story *about* beneath the surface? Redemption? Betrayal? The cost of truth? The hunger for power? And what's the feel of the show? Is it gritty, stylish, hyper-realistic, emotionally raw, or full of genre flair? Think *Jack Ryan* vs *The Umbrella Academy*—same genre, totally different energy. Ask ChatGPT, "Summarize the underlying themes and emotional tone of a high-octane action-adventure series," and you'll clarify what's beating under all that adrenaline.

Include a **Visual and Stylistic Reference** section if you're aiming this at film or TV production. What does this world *look* and *feel* like? What films or shows is it in the family of? Are the action scenes grounded or wild? Are we using flashbacks, voiceover, or time jumps? You can even ask ChatGPT, "Create a visual style guide for a series that blends ancient ruins with near-future tech," and now your director or concept artist knows what world you're inviting them into.

Finally, you can include **The Big Picture**. Where is the story going in future seasons? Does it have an endgame? Will the villain evolve? Will new locations or factions be introduced? You don't need to script everything—just show that the series has legs. Ask ChatGPT, "Sketch out a three-season plan for an action series that starts with a lost city and ends with a global uprising," and you'll have the long-term vision that networks and streamers love to see.

The great thing is, once you've built your series bible with ChatGPT, you don't just have a document—you have a launch-pad. You can use it to pitch, to stay on track as you write, or to hand off to collaborators. It becomes the spine of your entire creative project.

So if you've got the story, the characters, and the pilot... don't stop there.

Turn it into something bigger.

Something ongoing.

Something *ready to go*.

Because the moment you finish your series bible—

You're not just writing an action story anymore.

You're creating a *world worth returning to*.

Again. And again. And again.

Turning the Story into a Novel and a Screenplay

You've done the work. The characters are fleshed out, the world feels alive, the plot is tight, and you've got explosive action threaded through real emotional stakes. Whether you wrote the story as a fast-paced outline, a complete pilot, or a one-day action-adventure sprint using ChatGPT, now comes the next move—the one that turns this idea into a flexible powerhouse: adapting it into both a **novel** and a **screenplay**. Two formats. Two audiences. Same core story, told through different lenses.

Here's the good news you don't have to choose between the two. In fact, the best way to future-proof your story is to build it in both forms. That way, you've got a book that readers can sink into *and* a screenplay that's ready to pitch, submit, or even shoot. And thanks to ChatGPT, adapting the story across both formats doesn't take months—it can happen fast, clean, and creatively, with a little guidance and a lot of momentum.

Let's start with turning your story into a **novel**.

A novel gives you the chance to expand your action-adventure story in ways screenplays can't. You can dive into a character's internal world, explore backstory, play with pacing, and give the reader the full sensory experience of every setting, every breath, every twist. You're not limited by page count, budget, or camera angles—only by your ability to write clearly and keep the reader hooked.

Take your outline, beat sheet, or pilot script and say to ChatGPT, "Expand this action sequence into a prose novel scene with internal thoughts and sensory detail." You'll get vivid, cinematic prose that pulls the reader into the experience. Then keep layering. Add emotion. Description. World-building. Ask for deeper monologues or sub-textual reactions during action. Flesh out side characters. Include flashbacks, personal thoughts, and motivations. You're giving the reader the full ride, not just the visible one.

Novels are about **immersion**. That means building scenes with atmosphere, tone, and internal tension—not just visible stakes. When writing your novel version, you can slow down in the right places. You can have quieter beats, let characters think and feel, and dive deep into motivations that might only be hinted at on screen. Ask ChatGPT, "Write a reflective moment for my action hero after barely escaping death," and now your character arc breathes inside the action.

But what about turning that story into a **screenplay**?

This is where things flip. A screenplay is lean, stripped down, and made to be *seen and heard*, not felt in a reader's mind. It's not about what a character is thinking—it's about what they *do*. That internal monologue from the novel? In a screenplay, it needs to be a line of dialogue, a look, or a gesture. And that sprawling paragraph of rich description? It needs to become something visual and concise.

You're now writing a blueprint for directors, actors, producers, and the camera. The formatting changes: scene headings, action lines, character names in caps, dialogue centered. No prose flourishes. No lengthy exposition. Just movement and moments. Ask ChatGPT, "Turn this novel scene into screenplay format with clear slug lines and action blocks," and you'll get a properly formatted draft that looks like it came from Final Draft.

In screenwriting, you live on the surface—but that doesn't mean it's shallow. You just let subtext carry the weight. "She hesitates at the door" tells the audience more than a full page of internal debate. A single line like "You always did like blowing things up" can carry history, humor, and tension all at once. Ask ChatGPT, "Rewrite this internal conflict as subtextual dialogue between the hero and antagonist," and your screenplay gains emotional depth without losing pace.

The great part about writing both formats is that **they inform each other**. The screenplay teaches you how to tighten the novel. The novel helps you find the emotional truth inside the screenplay. You might even write both in parallel—using your beat sheet to guide structure and then choosing which format to write scene-by-scene.

Let's say you've written a killer chapter where your hero escapes a collapsing mountain fortress. Now ask ChatGPT, "Adapt this chapter into a 3-minute action sequence in screenplay format." Then flip it: "Now expand the screenplay into a novel chapter with emotional reflection and backstory." You're generating both versions from the same story core, quickly and efficiently, without losing any of the energy.

When you're done, you'll have a **dual asset**—a novel ready to publish or self-publish, and a script ready to pitch, submit to contests, or film yourself. That's rare air. Most people write one or the other. But when you write both, you're thinking like a creator, not just a writer.

And don't worry about being too perfect right out the gate. Use ChatGPT as your rewriter, your format fixer, your dialogue puncher-upper. Ask things like:

"Improve this fight dialogue to sound more cinematic."

"Cut this novel scene to 60 seconds of visual action."

"Make this screenplay description more punchy and professional."

You're never stuck. You're always iterating.

So take the story you just brought to life—this world you built, this hero you shaped—and give it two lives.

Write the novel that dives deep.

Write the script that hits hard.

And let the story travel both roads.

Because sometimes the best way to make your idea unstoppable...

Is to make it **two stories in one**.

Fixing Pacing and Plot Holes with ChatGPT's Help

There's nothing more frustrating than getting halfway through your action-adventure story and realizing something just feels... off. Maybe the pacing drags. Maybe a scene comes too early or too late. Maybe a character makes a choice that doesn't make sense, or a twist lands flat because you didn't set it up properly. Welcome to the land of pacing problems and plot holes. The good news is, you're not stuck there. With ChatGPT in your corner, you can diagnose, repair, and even supercharge your story without tearing the whole thing apart.

First, let's talk pacing. Pacing is about how your story *feels* as it unfolds. Is it dragging when it should be sprinting? Is it jumping too fast through key emotional beats? Is your middle act sagging like a hammock on a windless day? These are signs your rhythm is off. Luckily, they're fixable.

Start by identifying your story's flow. You can literally paste your outline or chapter list into ChatGPT and say, "Analyze this story structure and tell me where the pacing slows down or feels uneven." ChatGPT will walk through your beats and point out where things are front-loaded, where there's too little conflict, or where your tension dips for too long without a purpose.

A classic mistake in action-adventure is trying to pack too much into the beginning. If your story opens with a car chase, a shootout, a betrayal, a dream sequence, and a backstory dump—all within the first ten pages—you're burning your fuel too fast. Ask ChatGPT, "Help me rebalance the first act so it builds tension more gradually," and you'll get a sequence of beats that hook without overwhelming.

On the flip side, if your second act feels like it's circling the drain, you probably need more stakes, surprises, or reversals. This is where the plot should thicken—not stall. Ask ChatGPT, "Suggest ways to raise the stakes in the middle of my story involving an ancient artifact and rival treasure hunters," and suddenly you're back in motion.

Now let's move to the other monster: **plot holes**.

Plot holes are those logical gaps or inconsistencies that break immersion. You'll know you've hit one when your own brain goes, "Wait, didn't they just say...?" or "Why wouldn't they just...?" These are the gaps in cause and effect, in character behavior, or in your story's internal logic.

Instead of scanning every page manually, use ChatGPT like a narrative detective. Copy a scene—or the whole story outline—and say, "Can you find any inconsistencies or plot holes in this story summary?" ChatGPT will pick up on contradictions, missing explanations, or character decisions that don't line up with their established goals or fears.

A great trick is to get specific. Ask:

"Does it make sense for the villain to spare the hero in this scene based on earlier events?"

"Would the hero realistically know this information at this point in the story?"

"Is the twist in chapter ten properly foreshadowed in earlier scenes?"

ChatGPT will either confirm your logic or suggest tweaks to tighten the thread. Sometimes all it takes is one line of added dialogue or a quick flashback to fix what looked like a giant hole.

Here's a common one: a character magically appears in a faraway location without explanation. Instead of rewriting entire scenes, ask ChatGPT, "How can I justify this character's arrival without changing the plot?" You'll get smart solutions—an intercepted radio message, a planted GPS tracker, a backup plan previously hinted at. All small edits with big fixes.

Pacing and plot holes often go hand in hand. If your climax feels rushed, you may have skipped steps. If your emotional scenes fall flat, maybe your character arc is missing a key moment of growth earlier on. ChatGPT can help you scan the arc and say, "Suggest a missing beat that would make the climax feel more emotionally earned."

You can also fix micro-pacing. If a scene feels like it drags, say, "Rewrite this action sequence to move faster and feel more intense," or "Condense this exposition into a shorter, punchier paragraph." ChatGPT doesn't just point out problems—it patches them in seconds, giving you variations to pick from.

Sometimes the issue isn't just what's in the story—it's what *isn't*. That missing scene. That skipped consequence. That unaddressed clue. Ask, "What scenes might be missing from this plot to make it feel complete and satisfying?" and you'll uncover blind spots that your reader would've noticed—before they had the chance to.

And for the moments when you know something's wrong, but you can't quite name it? Try this:

"Tell me what's not working in this scene and how I can fix it for clarity, pace, or logic."

You might be surprised how clearly ChatGPT reads your material and diagnoses the issue.

The best part? None of this requires a rewrite from scratch. You can keep your core intact. You're simply patching the boat, tightening the ropes, tuning the engine.

Because pacing problems and plot holes aren't signs of a broken story.

They're signs you're close—and just need a second pair of eyes to *see it right*.

And with ChatGPT as your fixer, editor, and narrative engineer, you're never really writing alone.

You're tuning the ride for maximum thrill—and making sure it doesn't fall apart at 90 miles an hour.

The Final Polish Before You Hit "Publish"

You've done the heavy lifting. The action sequences are tight. The dialogue crackles. The pacing flows like a fuse burning toward something explosive. You've revised the twists, patched the plot holes, added depth to your characters, and maybe even adapted your story into both a novel and a screenplay. Now comes the last part—the deceptively simple but absolutely crucial moment before you hit that glowing "Publish" button. It's time for the final polish.

This isn't about rewriting your entire story. It's about zooming in, refining, and cleaning up those last remaining rough edges that could dull the impact of all the brilliant work you've done. And when you're up against time, pressure, or just plain exhaustion, ChatGPT becomes your final set of sharp eyes—your instant editor, your last-chance dialogue fixer, your voice checker, and your story whisperer.

Start with **consistency**. Even the best stories can suffer from tiny continuity problems. A gun that's out of bullets magically fires again. A character forgets something they knew two chapters ago. The villain's plan suddenly doesn't add up. You can ask ChatGPT, "Check this story for inconsistencies or logic gaps across character behavior and plot events," and it'll walk through your chapters or scenes like a detective looking for narrative fingerprints.

Next, focus on **voice and tone**. By this point, your story should have a clear identity. Is it gritty and grounded? Fast and pulpy? Witty and modern? You want your language, your dialogue, and even your action description to all live in that same world. Ask ChatGPT, "Review this chapter and adjust the tone to match the fast-paced, cinematic style of the rest of the story," and you'll avoid those awkward shifts that pull readers out of the zone.

Then tackle **dialogue polish**. Dialogue is where a lot of last-minute problems hide—lines that sound a little too stiff, explanations that drag, emotional beats that don't quite land. This is the time to trim the fat, punch up the banter, or rewrite that one line you know should hit harder. Try: "Punch up this exchange with more tension and subtext," or "Make this confrontation sharper and more in character," and let ChatGPT fine-tune the moments that count.

Pay special attention to **openings and endings**. That first scene? It has to *grab*. Not just with action, but with intrigue. Stakes. Voice. Ask ChatGPT, "Rewrite my opening paragraph to be more gripping and cinematic," and you'll have three or four alternatives in seconds. The ending? It should feel earned, even if it's not tied up with a bow. You want to leave your audience satisfied, stunned, or stirred. Try, "Suggest three alternative final lines that leave a lasting impression," and you'll get options that might be stronger than what you originally wrote.

Another area to polish is your **action description**. Does it flow? Is it easy to visualize? Are there too many mechanical movements—"he ducked, rolled, jumped"—with no sensory impact? Ask ChatGPT, "Rewrite this action sequence with more visual clarity and emotional intensity," and you'll turn stiff choreography into a page-turning thrill.

While you're at it, run a **line edit pass**. This is where you look for repeated words, clunky sentences, awkward phrasing, or lines that could be trimmed or reworded. You can paste a scene and say, "Rewrite this to be tighter and more polished without changing the meaning," and ChatGPT will cut the fat without touching the flavor.

Then, focus on **readability and pacing**. Maybe your paragraphs are too long. Maybe you've got five dialogue-free pages in a row. Maybe your exposition bogs down an otherwise great chapter. Ask, "Break this scene into shorter, punchier paragraphs for better pacing," or "Simplify this exposition to keep momentum without losing information," and your pacing will sharpen immediately.

And don't skip **title and tagline** work. A great story deserves a killer title. Ask ChatGPT, "Suggest alternative titles for a fast-paced action-adventure story about a rogue agent racing to stop a global catastrophe," and you'll get a list that might spark the perfect fit. Do the same for your tagline or back-cover blurb. "Make this story summary more compelling and dramatic for readers browsing online" turns your synopsis into a sales hook.

If you're self-publishing, this is also the time to prep your **final file**—clean formatting, consistent chapter headings, and scene breaks. Ask ChatGPT, "Help me organize this manuscript into standard novel formatting for Kindle or PDF export," and it can walk you through the checklist.

And finally, the **gut check**. That one last read. Not as the writer, but as the *reader*. Take a break, then come back and read it like it's your favorite book or show in the world. If a line doesn't sit right—ask ChatGPT to rewrite it. If something feels rushed—expand it. If something feels flat—elevate it. You don't have to fix everything at once. But you do owe it to yourself to give the story the final attention it deserves.

Because once you hit "Publish," it's no longer just a document on your screen. It's *out there*. It's a book. A screenplay. A pilot. A calling card. A statement.

And it should feel *ready*.

So polish it until it shines.

Tighten it until it hums.

Feel that little jolt of pride before you send it into the world.

And if you ever feel like it's not quite there?

Just ask ChatGPT:

"What's the one last thing I can do to make this story unforgettable?"

Then breathe in.

Hit publish.

And let it fly.

Selling Your Action-Adventure Script or Book

You've written the thing. It's polished, it's powerful, and it punches like a cinematic haymaker. Your characters are compelling, the pacing's tight, the action rips across the page, and the climax leaves people breathless. Now comes the next big mission—selling it. Whether you've got a screenplay ready for the screen or a novel begging to land in readers' hands, getting your action-adventure story into the marketplace takes more than just good writing. It takes smart strategy, relentless energy, and a willingness to pitch like your story depends on it—because it does.

Let's start with the **screenplay path**. If your goal is to see your story brought to life on the big or small screen, you need to get it in front of people who can say yes: producers, managers, agents, and decision-makers at production companies. Before you even think about selling, make sure your script is formatted professionally. If you haven't already, ask ChatGPT, "Format this scene according to industry screenplay standards," or "Give feedback on pacing and clarity in this script excerpt," and get it production-ready.

Now you need a **logline**—a one or two sentence pitch that nails the hook of your story. Think of it like a movie trailer compressed into a sentence. Something like: *A burned-out treasure hunter is pulled back into the game when a deadly cult surfaces, seeking a lost relic that could rewrite history.* Ask ChatGPT, "Generate ten logline variations for a high-stakes action-adventure film," and fine-tune one that's punchy, tight, and intriguing.

Next up: **query letters and pitch emails**. If you're reaching out to agents or production companies, you'll need a concise, respectful, and professional email that introduces yourself, pitches your project, and offers to send the full script. Ask ChatGPT, "Write a professional query letter for an action-adventure screenplay about a rogue ex-agent uncovering a global conspiracy," and you'll have a clean, ready-to-send version that makes a solid first impression.

You can submit to **screenwriting competitions** too—many of which serve as gateways into the industry. Look for respected ones like The Nicholl Fellowship, Final Draft Big Break, PAGE Awards, or Screencraft's Action & Adventure contest. A finalist placement in a major comp can put your script on the radar of people looking for new material. Ask ChatGPT, "Help me write a compelling script synopsis for a competition entry," and you'll have a short pitch that sells the heart of your story.

There's also the **screenwriting platform route**. Sites like Coverfly, The Black List, and Stage 32 let you host your script, get feedback, and connect with professionals. Just make sure your project stands out on the page. Ask ChatGPT, "Rewrite the opening scene of my script to make it more visually dynamic," and you'll level up your hook instantly.

Now let's shift to the **novel route**. If your story's been written or adapted as a novel, your first big decision is: traditional publishing or self-publishing?

For **traditional**, you'll need a literary agent, which means sending query letters and sample chapters. Just like with screenplays, you'll need a killer pitch and a polished manuscript. Ask ChatGPT, "Write a compelling query letter for an action-adventure novel in the style of Clive Cussler," and you'll get the tone just right. Research agents who represent action, thriller, or adventure books, and personalize each query. Don't mass-blast—target and tailor.

If you're going **indie**, you're in control—but that means you wear every hat: author, publisher, marketer. Thankfully, ChatGPT can help with every one of them. For your cover, create a title and tagline combo that screams adventure. Ask ChatGPT, "Suggest a bold, marketable title for a self-published action-adventure novel," and let the ideas roll. For the blurb, say, "Write a back-cover blurb that sells this story like a bestselling thriller." It should create curiosity, tease conflict, and give readers a reason to click "Buy Now."

Once the book is out, it's time for **marketing**. Build a presence on platforms like Amazon, Goodreads, Instagram, TikTok (yes, #BookTok is real), and Facebook. Ask ChatGPT, "Help me write five attention-grabbing social media posts to promote my action-adventure book," and you'll get short, shareable content that actually sells. Set up a basic website. Collect emails. Offer a sample chapter. Run promotions. Book blog tours. Leave no stone unturned.

If you've got both a screenplay and a novel version of your story, even better. Some producers love seeing source material first. You can lead with the novel and then mention the adapted script. Or vice versa. Having both in your arsenal shows that you're not just a writer—you're a *creator*. You understand story across platforms, and that makes you stand out.

Remember, **selling a story takes persistence**. You'll get ignored. You'll get rejections. You might even get notes that feel like setbacks. But the difference between writers who get published or produced and writers who don't? The ones who succeed *keep going*. They refine the pitch. They send the next email. They write the next thing. And every "no" brings them closer to the "yes."

So ask ChatGPT anything, anytime.

"Who are top agents for action-adventure novels?"

"How do I write a 90-second pitch for a Netflix-style series?"

"What should my book's Amazon description look like for maximum clicks?"

Because once your story is finished, it deserves to be *seen*.

And if you've got the courage to write it, you've got the guts to sell it too.

Your story's not just a manuscript.

It's a ticket—to bookstores, screens, streamers, or studios.

So get out there.

Start pitching.

Keep going.

Because one yes changes everything.

You Wrote an Action-Adventure Story in a Day—Now What?

Take a breath. You did it. You wrote a full-blown action-adventure story—beginning, middle, and explosive end—in just one day. Whether you wrote a screenplay, a novel, or both, you took an idea that started as a spark and turned it into a finished draft. That alone is a major victory. Most people never even start. You didn't just start—you *finished*. But now that the adrenaline is settling and the dust has cleared, a question hits you: *Now what?*

Here's the answer: now you refine, repackage, and release. You step into the second phase of the journey. The one where your story stops living only in your head and starts making its way into the world—whether that's to readers, publishers, agents, producers, contests, or streaming platforms. What you do *after* the draft is just as important as writing it. Because finishing a story in one day is impressive. But making it last? That's the real adventure.

Let's start with what you should do *right now*—today, if possible. Save your draft in multiple places. Don't just trust your computer or your cloud. Back it up. Email it to yourself. Throw it in Google Drive, Dropbox, an external hard drive—anywhere safe. You just created something valuable, and it deserves protection.

Next, walk away from it. Not forever. Just for a few hours. Maybe even a day or two. Give your brain some space. Let the story settle in your subconscious. You'll see it more clearly when you return, and when you do, you're going to wear a different hat: *editor*. This is where ChatGPT becomes your secret weapon. Say, "Read this draft and help me find weak spots in pacing, character motivation, and dialogue," and you'll instantly get feedback you can use to level it up without starting over.

If you wrote a novel draft, start breaking it into chapters and checking for consistency in tone, world-building, and arc progression. If you wrote a screenplay, do a format check. Make sure your scene headings are clear, your action lines are lean, and your dialogue is tight. Ask ChatGPT, "Help me format this screenplay scene correctly," or "Turn this scene into a punchier, more visual moment," and polish becomes painless.

Once your first pass of editing is complete, create versions. A clean manuscript. A PDF. A screenplay in Final Draft format or a standard .doc version of your novel. You now have material that can be submitted, shared, or published.

Now it's time to decide your direction.

If you're aiming for **traditional publishing or representation**, you'll want to prepare query letters, synopses, and loglines. Ask ChatGPT, "Write a professional query letter for my action-adventure novel," and you'll have a template that's clean, confident, and attention-grabbing. Then start submitting to agents or contests that specialize in action, adventure, or thrillers. Be strategic. Keep track of submissions. Don't mass-blast—*target*.

If you're going **indie or self-publishing**, your next steps are practical. You'll need a cover (ChatGPT can help you conceptualize it), a compelling back-cover blurb ("Write me a dynamic book blurb in the tone of Matthew Reilly or James Rollins"), and clean formatting for Kindle, paperback, and ebook platforms. You can have it on Amazon in less than a week.

If you're thinking **screenplay**, look into contests, pitch platforms, and coverage services. Ask ChatGPT, "List ten reputable screenplay contests for action-adventure scripts," or "Give me a short pitch for my script about a covert agent uncovering an ancient weapon." You'll be amazed how quickly you can start packaging your story for industry eyes.

But don't stop there.

You've already proven that you can create a full story in a day. Now think bigger. Can this story become a series? A trilogy? A universe? Could it be a graphic novel? A podcast? A video game pitch? ChatGPT can help you scale the idea up: "Turn this story into a three-book action series with distinct character arcs," or "Build a show bible for an action-adventure streaming series based on this pilot." The bones are there—you just need to build on them.

And if the idea of revisiting this world doesn't excite you, that's okay too. Move on. Take what you learned. Use what worked. Leave what didn't. Then write another story in a day. And another. You'll get faster. Sharper. Smarter. And soon, you'll have a portfolio of finished, tested stories—each one tighter, more confident, and more marketable than the last.

You've already beaten the hardest part: *the blank page*.

Now it's about showing up again. Crafting new characters. Trying new structures. Challenging yourself to go deeper or bolder or stranger. And yes, ChatGPT can be there for every single story. As co-writer, editor, sounding board, and production assistant. Ask it anything. Trust it to push you. Let it make suggestions, then make them your own.

Because the story you wrote in one day? That wasn't a fluke.

That was proof.

Proof you've got the creativity, the vision, and the momentum to write fast, write well, and write again.

So now what?

Now you *keep going*.

One day. One story. One adventure at a time.

Examples of ChatGPT Prompts for Action-Adventure Story Ideas

One of the greatest superpowers you now have as a writer is the ability to generate fresh, exciting, and high-concept ideas anytime you want—using ChatGPT as your creative engine. Action-adventure stories thrive on originality mixed with timeless tropes: a daring hero, a powerful objective, an exotic setting, an insurmountable obstacle. But coming up with *fresh* takes on these elements can feel tough when the blank page is staring back at you. That's where the right prompt can change everything.

In this chapter, you'll find a vault of practical, customizable prompts you can feed into ChatGPT to generate action-adventure story ideas, character concepts, missions, villains, set-pieces, twists, worlds, and more. Use them to spark new stories, rework stuck drafts, or remix genres. These prompts are flexible—just change a few words, and you'll get entirely new ideas on demand.

Let's start with **story concept prompts**—the ones that deliver complete plot frameworks in a few lines:

"Give me ten original action-adventure story ideas involving a lost civilization and a rogue archaeologist."

"Create a plot outline for a high-stakes action story set on a space station being taken over by mercenaries."

"Generate five action-adventure concepts that mix modern tech with ancient mythology."

"Pitch a story where a group of unlikely heroes must recover a stolen artifact before it triggers a global disaster."

Want to focus on your **hero**? Try:

"Invent a compelling action-adventure protagonist with a dark past and a unique skill set. Include name, background, and personal stakes."

"Give me a female hero who was once a spy but is now pulled back into a mission against her will."

"Create a morally grey action hero who's after the same treasure as the antagonist—but for very different reasons."

Looking to develop **villains** with bite? Try:

"Describe an action-adventure antagonist who believes they're saving the world—even if millions die."

"Invent a powerful villain who was once a friend or mentor to the hero."

"Give me five original villain ideas for an action story set in a post-apocalyptic desert."

Need some **settings** to match the tone of your story? Prompt:

"List ten exotic or dangerous locations perfect for an action-adventure story, with a short description of each."

"Describe an ancient temple hidden in Antarctica that guards a terrifying secret."

"Create a futuristic city built inside a volcano, used by criminals to trade stolen artifacts."

For epic **set pieces and missions**, try:

"Generate a high-stakes chase scene involving a motorcycle, a crumbling bridge, and a thunderstorm."

"Describe a mission where the hero must infiltrate a fortress disguised as a sacred monastery."

"Write a thrilling escape sequence from an underwater cave filling with explosive gas."

Want character interaction and **conflict-driven dynamics**?

"Write a tense dialogue between a hero and an enemy who must temporarily work together."

"Give me a conversation where a sidekick realizes the hero is lying about their past."

"Create a scene where the villain offers the hero a deal that challenges their morals."

Looking for clever **twists and story turns**?

"Suggest five unexpected twists that could happen in an action-adventure story about a lost treasure."

"What's a third-act betrayal that completely flips the hero's mission?"

"Give me a plot twist where the real villain has been helping the hero all along."

Maybe you want to mash genres—go wild with **action-comedy**, **sci-fi adventure**, or **historical thrillers**:

"Create a time-travel action-adventure story where the hero must stop a war before it starts in 1920s Paris."

"Give me a buddy-cop action comedy idea set inside a virtual reality world gone rogue."

"Pitch an action-adventure novel with a steampunk twist and a pirate crew searching for an airborne fortress."

And when you're totally blank and just need to shake things up:

"Give me five wild, unexpected mashups of genres for an action-adventure story."

"What's a high-concept logline for an action-adventure story you've never seen before?"

"Tell me the most outrageous treasure-hunting plot you can think of—and make it work."

Use these prompts as launchpads. Feed them into ChatGPT and then play with the results. Ask for expansions. Change the setting. Flip the character's gender. Add a betrayal. Remove the artifact and insert an ancient curse instead. Every result can be pushed further.

Here's a simple three-step system for generating endless material with prompts:

1. **Ask for ten ideas** related to your chosen concept (like "hero must infiltrate an enemy stronghold").
2. **Pick one** that excites you and say, "Expand this into a 3-act story with character arcs and major set pieces."
3. **Start writing**, or ask ChatGPT to help develop key scenes, structure, or even write a first draft with you.

The goal is not just to get one idea. It's to keep the ideas *flowing*. The more you prompt, the more connections you'll see—and the faster you'll be able to move from spark to story.

You don't need to wait for inspiration anymore.

You can generate it on demand.

So next time you're staring at the screen and wondering where to begin, just ask:

"Hey ChatGPT, give me something wild. Let's write an adventure."

And then... buckle up.

Because adventure is only ever one prompt away.

Examples of ChatGPT Prompts for Action-Adventure Settings and World Building

In action-adventure storytelling, setting is more than just a backdrop. It's a character. It's mood, challenge, mystery, and possibility. Whether your hero is leaping from rooftops in a war-torn city, diving through ancient underwater ruins, or navigating a jungle hiding centuries-old traps, the *world* they move through is what gives the story depth and energy. Great world-building turns ordinary missions into unforgettable epics. And with ChatGPT, you don't have to spend weeks creating rich, dynamic settings—you can build immersive worlds in minutes.

In this chapter, you'll find tons of flexible, creative prompts you can use to ask ChatGPT for help crafting vivid, action-packed settings. These prompts are designed to give you **instant inspiration**, fully-formed ideas, or building blocks you can stack together to make unique, high-stakes environments for your characters to explore, escape, or destroy.

Let's kick off with **setting generation prompts**:

"Create five unique and dangerous locations for an action-adventure story involving a secret global organization."

"Describe an abandoned research facility in the Arctic that holds a long-buried secret."

"Invent an underground city hidden beneath the ruins of Pompeii, complete with its own technology, culture, and defenses."

"Generate three ancient temples, each with a distinct design style and trap system, hidden across different continents."

Want **historical** or **mythological locations** with a twist?

"Give me a reimagined version of the Library of Alexandria that was never destroyed, just hidden from the world."

"Describe a secret island that appears only once every century and contains artifacts from lost civilizations."

"Create an ancient battlefield turned cursed zone where weapons still move as if the war never ended."

"Build a mountain fortress that once belonged to a forgotten empire and now serves as the villain's base."

How about **urban environments**?

"Design a gritty, futuristic city where illegal treasure hunters operate under the radar of an authoritarian regime."

"Describe a crumbling European city built over layers of ancient catacombs and forgotten tunnels."

"Give me a modern metropolis with hidden entrances to a parallel underground society that protects the world's secrets."

If you're building out a **global adventure**, use:

"Create a world map concept for a globe-trotting action-adventure story involving five major locations—each with a different climate, culture, and mystery."

"List five exotic, remote places where a legendary artifact might be hidden. Include natural hazards and local legends."

"Describe a network of temples linked across continents, each containing a piece of a puzzle leading to the ultimate treasure."

Need **specific environments** for chase scenes or confrontations?

"Give me a vertical action setting—something like a cliffside monastery or skyscraper under attack—perfect for climbing, falling, and narrow escapes."

"Design a desert canyon system used by smugglers with hidden caves and narrow paths for ambushes."

"Describe a fog-filled jungle swamp where enemies can disappear in seconds and sound is distorted."

Want your world to have **rules, factions, and history**?

"Build the world for an action-adventure story set in a society where ancient ruins are controlled by corporate scavenger guilds."

"Describe the mythology, local superstitions, and historical wars that shaped a hidden island off the coast of Japan."

"Create a secret society that has protected a powerful artifact for 2,000 years. Where is their stronghold, and how is it defended?"

"Build the background for a rogue nation built on ancient technology and surrounded by impenetrable mountains."

Looking to mix in **fantasy, science fiction, or alternate history**?

"Design a world where World War II never ended, and treasure hunters uncover tech hidden by fallen empires."

"Describe a post-apocalyptic wasteland where ancient cities have been swallowed by sand and the only maps are tattoos on outlaws."

"Create an alternate 1920s where explorers race to find mythical beasts before the black market gets to them."

Want a strong **sensory setting** to drop readers into the action?

"Describe a storm-ravaged coastline where the hero must recover a lost submarine—include sounds, sights, smells, and terrain."

"Write a vivid description of an abandoned space elevator covered in moss and home to scavengers."

"Give me a jungle scene where everything seems alive—and possibly watching."

You can also get **modular building blocks** like:

"List types of booby traps used in ancient ruins and how they might still be active."

"What cultural clues or architecture might reveal that an underground city was built by multiple civilizations?"

"Create five types of weather-based environmental challenges for a high-altitude mission."

Don't forget to experiment with **contrast and escalation**:

"Describe three contrasting locations the hero must cross—each with different dangers, technologies, and cultural tensions."

"Give me a progression of settings where the stakes escalate—from a coastal village to a deep-sea trench to a high-orbit weapons lab."

"Design a chase sequence that moves across rooftops, canals, and catacombs in Venice—each one introducing a new threat."

And if you're really stuck, just say:

"Surprise me with the most imaginative setting for an action-adventure story that you've never seen before."

With these prompts, you can generate entire **worlds** filled with tension, atmosphere, history, mystery, and danger. And the more you play with them—twist the genres, layer the stakes, remix the influences—the more unique your action-adventure story becomes.

So if you want your hero running, climbing, dodging, or discovering somewhere unforgettable...

Just tell ChatGPT where you want to go.

And it'll open the door.

Every time.

Examples of ChatGPT Prompts for Action-Adventure Character Ideas

A great action-adventure story is only as strong as the characters running, fighting, sneaking, stealing, climbing, surviving, or saving the day at the heart of it. Your protagonist might be a rogue archaeologist, a betrayed spy, a hardened mercenary, or a rookie thrown into chaos. Your villains might be brilliant masterminds, obsessed collectors, warlords with wounded pride, or charming traitors. Side characters carry tech, crack jokes, hold secrets, or sacrifice themselves at the last moment. Every single one matters—and ChatGPT can help you generate unforgettable character ideas on demand.

In this chapter, you'll find a ton of highly usable, customizable ChatGPT prompts that will instantly spark character ideas for any kind of action-adventure story, no matter the setting, tone, or genre twist you're working with. Use them to create heroes, villains, sidekicks, traitors, mentors, rival teams, ancient guardians, and everyone in between.

Let's start with **hero prompts**—the beating heart of your adventure:

"Create a compelling action-adventure hero who's a disgraced former military officer with a personal vendetta."

"Give me five protagonist ideas for a globetrotting treasure-hunter story. Each one should have a different personality, background, and flaw."

"Invent a reluctant action hero who's only in it for the money—until they discover something worth fighting for."

"Build a character profile for a female marine biologist who accidentally uncovers a conspiracy while exploring underwater ruins."

"Design an action hero who used to be a villain. What changed, and what still haunts them?"

Need some **unique action-adventure villains**?

"Create a charismatic antagonist who believes they're saving the world by recovering a lost weapon."

"Give me five villain concepts for a high-stakes jungle expedition story. One should be a rival treasure hunter, one a local warlord, one a backstabbing ally."

"Describe a villain who was once the protagonist's mentor, now obsessed with completing a mission at any cost."

"Invent a villain who never appears in person until the end, but manipulates everything from the shadows."

For **sidekicks, support characters, and rival teams**, try:

"Create a loyal but unpredictable sidekick for a hero who doesn't trust anyone. Include background, specialty, and secret motivation."

"Invent a team of rogue adventurers—each one with a different skill set, personality, and weakness."

"Give me five supporting characters for an action-adventure story about a lost city—one should be comic relief, one a romantic interest, one a double agent."

"Describe a local guide character who knows more than they're letting on and has their own hidden agenda."

Want some **morally ambiguous or twist potential**?

"Invent an action hero who might actually be the villain in disguise."

"Create a morally ambiguous mercenary character who will help anyone—for the right price."

"Give me a trio of characters where one will betray the others—but don't reveal who until late in the story."

"Design a rival character who mirrors the hero's skills and past, making the final confrontation deeply personal."

Looking to develop deeper **character arcs**?

"Build a character arc for a hardened assassin who learns to value life over victory through a dangerous mission."

"Outline the emotional journey of a hero who fails to save their team and must carry that guilt into the next mission."

"Describe how a villain character could gradually turn into an anti-hero across three acts."

"Give me a redemption arc for a side character who betrayed the group but comes back at the most crucial moment."

You can also go wild with **genre mashups and creative types**:

"Invent five unusual action-adventure protagonists: one should be a monk, one a hacker, one a former thief, one a disgraced archaeologist, and one a kid raised in isolation."

"Describe a steampunk-era heroine who flies a mechanical airship and is being hunted by royal bounty hunters."

"Create a post-apocalyptic scavenger who finds an ancient map that others would kill for."

"Generate a sci-fi soldier sent to recover lost technology in an alien jungle filled with traps and mutated fauna."

Or build a full **character sheet** using prompts like:

"Give me a full character profile for an action-adventure hero. Include name, appearance, personality, skills, backstory, flaw, mission, and secret."

"Build a detailed villain profile for a corporate-backed explorer who will stop at nothing to find the lost city of gold."

"Write a dossier for a mysterious mercenary with a false identity and ties to the villain's past."

"Create a team of five specialists—explosives expert, linguist, survivalist, tech operator, and ex-spy—assembled for a covert jungle op."

You can even prompt for **dialogue, introductions, or character scenes**:

"Write an intense dialogue scene where the hero first meets the antagonist, pretending not to know who they really are."

"Write a monologue from a villain explaining why they believe their cause is just—even if it causes mass destruction."

"Give me an action scene that shows my character's personality through how they survive an ambush."

"Write the moment when a new ally joins the team and immediately causes tension."

And if you ever just want to surprise yourself:

"Invent the most original action-adventure character idea you can think of—and make it work in a grounded story."

"Give me a character I haven't seen before, but instantly want to follow into danger."

With these prompts, you'll never run out of characters to write. Heroes, villains, mentors, monsters, sidekicks, or turncoats—ChatGPT can deliver ideas faster than your brain can outline them. Keep refining. Keep remixing. And when something sparks?

Run with it.

Because in action-adventure, the world is wild—but the characters make it unforgettable.

Examples of ChatGPT Prompts for Action-Adventure Story Structure Ideas

The best action-adventure stories are more than just adrenaline-fueled chases, daring escapes, and thrilling fight scenes—they're built on solid, engaging story structures that keep readers or viewers hooked from the opening scene to the final showdown. Structure is your story's skeleton. It's the way you deliver rising tension, shocking twists, character growth, and ultimately, that satisfying ending that makes everything worth it.

The good news? You don't have to build that structure from scratch. With ChatGPT, you can generate, tweak, and even completely reinvent your story structure on the fly. Whether you're working with a classic three-act setup, a hero's journey, a non-linear format, or something entirely unique, the right prompt can unlock the framework your story needs.

This chapter is packed with practical and creative ChatGPT prompt ideas to help you structure your action-adventure story—quickly, cleanly, and powerfully.

Start with **basic story structure generation**:

"Create a 3-act action-adventure story structure with a clear inciting incident, midpoint twist, and climactic showdown."

"Outline an action-adventure story using the Save the Cat beat sheet structure."

"Give me a 5-act story structure for a high-stakes action story involving ancient treasure and a global conspiracy."

"Structure a 10-chapter action-adventure novel with a clear arc for the hero and escalating challenges."

Want to use **The Hero's Journey**?

"Apply the Hero's Journey framework to an action-adventure story about a rogue ex-soldier seeking a lost relic."

"Create a story structure using all 12 steps of the Hero's Journey, set in a post-apocalyptic wasteland."

"Break down an action-adventure story where the call to adventure is ignored, leading to massive consequences."

Try **genre mashup structures**:

"Give me a story structure that combines action-adventure with espionage—like Mission: Impossible meets Tomb Raider."

"Outline an action-adventure story structure with supernatural horror elements in the second act."

"Structure a modern-day treasure hunt story with a romantic subplot that peaks during the climax."

Need help with **episode or serialized structure**?

"Create a 6-episode arc for an action-adventure TV series where each episode reveals a piece of a larger mystery."

"Outline a serialized story structure for a 3-book action-adventure series with rising stakes in each book."

"Give me a pilot episode story structure that introduces the world, the hero, and a clear season-long threat."

Want to focus on **plot twists and reversals**?

"Insert a major plot twist at the midpoint that changes the hero's understanding of the mission."

"Build a structure where a character believed to be dead returns in Act Three."

"Outline a story where the villain wins the second act, and the hero must regroup in Act Three with fewer allies."

For **non-linear or experimental structures**, try:

"Create a non-linear structure for an action-adventure story told through flashbacks, present events, and one future glimpse."

"Build a time-loop action-adventure story structure where the hero learns a little more each time the loop resets."

"Give me a dual-timeline story structure—one timeline following a modern hero, the other a historical figure on the same mission."

Want structure that supports **character arcs**?

"Build a story structure around a hero who begins as selfish and slowly learns to sacrifice for the greater good."

"Give me a structure where the antagonist and protagonist have mirrored character arcs that collide in the finale."

"Create a plot structure that shows how the hero's flaw causes the midpoint failure, leading to a major growth moment before the climax."

Need help structuring **specific moments or acts**?

"What are the most important beats in Act One of an action-adventure story, and how can I structure them for momentum?"

"How should I structure the second act of an action-adventure story to avoid sagging and keep raising the stakes?"

"Give me three alternate structures for Act Three that lead to different types of climaxes—victory, sacrifice, or twist-ending."

Want to **build from your idea**?

"I have a story idea about a thief who must return a stolen artifact to stop a curse. Give me a story structure based on that."

"Help me create a structure for a story about a group of strangers brought together to stop a doomsday device."

"Give me a structure for a solo hero vs. nature survival story that transforms into a conspiracy thriller in the second half."

Or even use **structure prompts to inspire your next story**:

"Surprise me with an unusual action-adventure structure that doesn't use traditional acts but still works."

"Give me an outline for a story that starts with the final battle and works backward to explain how they got there."

"Create a structure for a story that alternates between high-octane action and quiet, emotional character scenes."

When you're ready to turn these structures into scenes, just say:

"Now build this structure into a beat sheet with 15 plot points."

"Expand this into a full chapter-by-chapter outline."

"Turn each major story beat into a scene prompt I can write from."

You don't need to be a master story architect. ChatGPT can be your co-plotter, outline builder, and structural editor—all in one. You just need to tell it what kind of ride you want to build—and it'll hand you the blueprint.

Because the truth is, even the wildest action-adventure needs structure to stay thrilling.

And now, structure is something you'll never have to guess at again.

Just prompt it. Shape it. Write it.

Then go set the world on fire—one scene at a time.

I hope you found inspiration within these pages. If you liked this book, please leave a review where you bought it. Thank you from the author.

www.ingramcontent.com/pod-product-compliance
Lightning Source LLC
LaVergne TN
LVHW082349200926
848481LV00012B/3504